The Law Commission
(LAW COM No 300)

INCHOATE LIABILITY FOR ASSISTING AND ENCOURAGING CRIME

*Presented to the Parliament of the United Kingdom by the Secretary of State
for Constitutional Affairs and Lord Chancellor by Command of Her Majesty
July 2006*

Cm 6878   London: The Stationery Office   £20.00

The Law Commission was set up by the Law Commissions Act 1965 for the purpose of promoting the reform of the law.

The Law Commissioners are:

> The Honourable Mr Justice Toulson, *Chairman*
> Professor Hugh Beale QC, FBA
> Mr Stuart Bridge
> Dr Jeremy Horder
> Mr Kenneth Parker QC

The Chief Executive of the Law Commission is Mr Steve Humphreys.

The Law Commission is located at Conquest House, 37-38 John Street, Theobalds Road, London WC1N 2BQ.

The terms of this report were agreed on 24 May 2006.

The text of this report is available on the Internet at:

http://www.lawcom.gov.uk

THE LAW COMMISSION

INCHOATE LIABILITY FOR ASSISTING AND ENCOURAGING CRIME

CONTENTS

PART 1
INTRODUCTION

1.1 The issue of criminal liability for encouraging or assisting another person to commit an offence is important, complex and difficult. It is important because it is very common for offences to involve two or more participants only some of whom are actual perpetrators of the offence as opposed to encouraging or assisting its commission.

1.2 The issue is also important because it is often the prime movers behind criminal ventures, for example drug or people traffickers, who take good care to distance themselves from the commission of the offences that they seek to encourage or assist. Recent advances in technology, together with the enhanced financial resources of career criminals, have facilitated this process.

1.3 This is the first of two reports in which we consider the circumstances in which a person ("D") ought to be criminally liable for encouraging or assisting another person ("P") to commit an offence. A substantial portion of this report focuses on what we consider to be a major defect of the common law. At common law if D *encourages* P to commit an offence that subsequently P does not commit or attempt to commit, D may nevertheless be criminally liable.[1] By contrast, if D *assists* P to commit an offence, D incurs no criminal liability at common law if subsequently P, for whatever reason, does not commit or attempt to commit the offence:

Example 1A

D, in return for payment, lends a van to P believing that P will use the van in order to commit a robbery. The police arrest P in connection with another matter before P can even attempt to commit the robbery.

D is not criminally liable despite the fact that he or she intended to bring about harm and, by lending the van to P, has manifested that intention. If, however, in addition to giving P the van, D had uttered words encouraging P to rob V, D would be guilty of incitement to commit robbery. The common law appears to treat words more seriously than deeds.[2] Yet, it might be thought that seeking to bring about harm by assisting a person to commit an offence is as culpable as seeking to do so by means of encouragement.[3]

---

[1] By virtue of having committed the common law offence of incitement.

[2] However, it would be wrong to try to rationalise the current law simply in terms of a dichotomy between words and deeds. It is not difficult to visualise cases where the assistance consists only of words, for example D, knowing that P intends to murder V, informs P as to V's current whereabouts.

[3] If P *does* commit the offence, the issue of D's liability is not dependent on whether he or she has encouraged P, on the one hand, or assisted P, on the other.

1.4   Increasingly, the police, through the gathering of intelligence, are able to identify preliminary acts of assistance by D before P commits or attempts to commit the principal offence. Yet, the common law only partially reflects this significant development. As a result, if D assists but does not encourage P to commit an offence, the police may have to forego at least some of the advantages of more sophisticated and effective methods of investigation by having to wait until P commits or attempts to commit the offence before they can proceed against D.[4]

1.5   In contrast to acts of assistance, if D encourages P to commit an offence which P does not go on to commit, D will be guilty of incitement provided he or she satisfies the fault element of the offence. However, the offence of incitement has a number of unsatisfactory features:

(1)   there is uncertainty as to whether it must be D's purpose that P should commit the offence that D is inciting;

(2)   the fault element of the offence has been distorted by decisions of the Court of Appeal.[5] These decisions have focused, wrongly, on the state of mind of P rather than on D's state of mind;

(3)   there is uncertainty as to whether and, if so, to what extent it is a defence to act in order to prevent the commission of an offence or to prevent or limit the occurrence of harm;

(4)   there is uncertainty as to the circumstances in which D is liable for inciting P to do an act which, if done by P, would not involve P committing an offence, for example because P is under the age of criminal responsibility or lacks a guilty mind;

(5)   the rules governing D's liability in cases where D incites P to commit an inchoate offence have resulted in absurd distinctions;

(6)   D may have a defence if the offence that he or she incites is impossible to commit whereas impossibility is not a defence to other inchoate offences, apart from common law conspiracies.

The offence of incitement is therefore in need of clarification and reform.

---

[4]   It is different if P and D agree to commit an offence. D and P are guilty of conspiracy and the offence is committed as soon as the agreement is concluded. Accordingly, the police can arrest and charge both P and D without having to wait for the offence to be committed or attempted.

[5]   *Curr* [1968] 2 QB 944; *Shaw* [1994] *Criminal Law Review* 365.

THE NATURE OF LIABILITY FOR ENCOURAGING OR ASSISTING THE COMMISSION OF OFFENCES

Principal offenders and accessories

1.6   When an offence is committed, the principal offender is a person who, with the requisite state of mind, perpetrates the conduct proscribed by the offence. An accessory is a person who, with the requisite state of mind, "aids, abets, counsels or procures"[6] the principal offender to perpetrate that conduct. There can be more than one principal offender and more than one accessory:

Example 1B

D and P agree to rob V. D holds a knife to V's throat while P takes £100 from V's pocket. D and P spend the money.

Example 1C

D and P agree to rob V. P approaches V while D keeps watch. P threatens V with a knife and takes £100 from V's pocket. D and P spend the money.

The conduct that the offence of robbery proscribes is the appropriation of property by the use or threatened use of force. In example 1B, P and D between them have perpetrated the proscribed conduct. Therefore, they are co-principals.

1.7   By contrast, in example 1C, P appropriates the property and threatens V with force. The only principal offender is P. However, by keeping watch, D has intentionally assisted P to perpetrate the forbidden conduct. The common law acknowledges that D has acted reprehensibly and merits punishment. By virtue of the common law doctrine of secondary liability,[7] D is an accessory to and guilty of robbery.

Secondary liability

1.8   The area of the criminal law that governs whether or not a person is guilty of an offence as an accessory is often described as the law of complicity and the liability of an accessory is often referred to as secondary liability. Secondary liability is a derivative form of liability in that D's liability derives from and is dependent on an offence committed by P. Although there are exceptions,[8] the general principle is that if P does not commit (or attempt to commit) the offence, D is not secondarily liable.

---

[6]   In relation to indictable offences, the language of the Accessories and Abettors Act 1861, s 8. Similar language is used in the Magistrates' Courts Act 1980, s 44 in relation to summary offences.

[7]   See para 1.8 below.

[8]   See A J Ashworth, *Principles of Criminal Law* (4th ed 2003) pp 435 to 438.

Inchoate liability

1.9   If P does not commit or attempt to commit the offence that D has encouraged or assisted, D may still be liable but only if his or her conduct amounts to an "inchoate" offence.

> **Example 1D**
>
> D encourages P to murder V. The police arrest P in connection with another matter just as P is about to leave home to murder V.

D does not incur secondary liability because no offence has been committed or attempted. However, as will become apparent, D is guilty of the inchoate offence of incitement (to murder).

1.10   On one view, D ought not to incur *any* criminal liability in example 1D because D's conduct has not resulted in any actual harm. On the other view, the *moral* quality of D's conduct is unaffected by the fact that P has not murdered or attempted to murder V. It was D's intention that actual harm should occur. Should D be exonerated, it might be thought that the law was "speaking with a strange moral voice".[9]

1.11   The common law developed three inchoate offences, that is offences that punish conduct not because it involves actual harm but because it enhances the prospect of actual harm occurring. The three offences were attempt,[10] conspiracy[11] and incitement.[12] They are freestanding offences although they always relate to a principal offence. Accordingly, the offences are charged by reference to the principal offence, for example attempted rape, conspiracy to rob and incitement to murder.

---

[9]   R A Duff, *Criminal Attempts* (1996) p 134.

[10] Attempt is now a statutory offence by virtue of the Criminal Attempts Act 1981, s 1(1).

[11] Conspiracy is also now a statutory offence by virtue of the Criminal Law Act 1977, s 1. However conspiracy as a common law offence has not been completely abolished. Conspiracy to defraud, conspiracy to corrupt public morals and conspiracy to outrage public decency remain common law offences.

[12] Although incitement remains a common law offence, Parliament has enacted many statutory offences of incitement. Examples include incitement to commit perjury contrary to the Perjury Act 1911, s 7(2); inciting acts of terrorism contrary to the Terrorism Act 2000, s 59; inciting offences relating to biological, chemical or nuclear weapons contrary to the Anti-Terrorism, Crime and Security Act 2001, s 50; inciting a child under 13 to engage in sexual activity contrary to the Sexual Offences Act 2003, s8.

1.12 Attempt is where P tries to commit an offence but fails to do so.[13] If P commits the attempt with D's encouragement or assistance, D is an accessory to P's attempt.[14] Therefore, if D urges P to murder V by discharging a firearm and P does so but misses the target, P and D are both guilty of attempted murder.

1.13 In contrast, the other two inchoate offences are offences that D commits:

(1) conspiracy consists of an agreement to commit an offence, for example D and P agree to assault V. The offence is committed by both D and P, as soon as the agreement is concluded, irrespective of whether any further steps are taken towards executing the agreement;[15]

(2) incitement is where D *encourages* P to commit an offence.[16] D is liable as soon as the encouragement comes to P's attention and thereafter it is irrelevant whether or not P acts on the encouragement. Accordingly, an act of encouragement, if accompanied by the requisite fault element, is an offence in its own right. This is why, in example 1D, D is guilty of incitement to murder.[17]

However, as we have explained,[18] there is no inchoate offence at common law for assisting a person to commit an offence if subsequently the offence is not committed or attempted.[19]

1.14 The three inchoate offences of attempt, conspiracy and incitement share two common features. First, in each case D incurs liability even though the principal offence is not committed. Secondly, they punish conduct that is one at least step removed from the commission of the principal offence.

---

[13] At common law the courts experienced problems in determining when mere preparation to commit the offence ceased and attempt to commit the offence began. At the risk of over-simplification, the issue confronting the courts was how proximate to the complete offence did D's actions have to be before they could constitute an attempt. The Criminal Attempts Act 1981, s 1(1) now provides that P must do an act that is "more than merely preparatory to the commission of the offence".

[14] *Hapgood and Wyatt* (1870) LR 1 CCR 221.

[15] Arguably, the mere requirement that there should be an agreement to commit an offence is a low threshold because it might be thought that D and P agreeing to commit an offence is not very different from D declaring an intention to commit an offence. At common law, the latter is not sufficient to ground criminal liability. On the other hand, where D and P agree to commit an offence there is an additional element, namely that of mutual encouragement.

[16] Incitement does not require mutual encouragement.

[17] In example 1D, if D and P had *agreed* to murder V, they would have been guilty of conspiracy to murder.

[18] Para 1.3 above.

[19] This view is challenged by P R Glazebrook, "Structuring the Criminal Code: Functional Approaches to Complicity, Incomplete Offences, and General Defences" in A P Simester and A T H Smith (eds), *Harm and Culpability* (1996) 195, 202. However, we are not aware of other scholars who share Mr Glazebrook's view.

1.15   In the consultation paper that the Commission published in 1993,[20] the Commission acknowledged that the current law of secondary and inchoate liability for encouraging or assisting others to commit crime was unsatisfactory.[21] As a solution, the Commission proposed "a new structure of statutory offences".[22] The proposals were based on the Commission's view that the nature of D's criminal liability for encouraging or assisting P to commit an offence is essentially inchoate in all cases.[23] On this view, D incurs the same liability irrespective of whether P subsequently commits or attempts to commit the principal offence.

1.16   The Commission put forward three main proposals. First, the common law offence of incitement should be abolished and replaced by a statutory offence of encouraging crime. Secondly, there should be a separate statutory offence imposing a general inchoate liability for assisting crime. Thirdly, subject to the possible retention of the common law doctrine of joint venture,[24] the doctrine of secondary liability should be abolished.

1.17   Thus, under the Commission's proposals, D's liability would always be inchoate irrespective of whether P went on to commit or attempt to commit the offence that D had encouraged or assisted:

Example 1E

D in return for payment lends P a jemmy that D believes P will use to burgle V's premises. P uses the jemmy to burgle V's premises.

Under the Commission's proposals, D would no longer be an accessory to and guilty of burglary. Instead, D would be guilty of assisting burglary.

1.18   The Commission's proposals were subjected to some searching criticism and no further work on the project was undertaken until 2002. The thrust of the criticism was that the Commission had been wrong to propose a scheme that involved the abolition of secondary liability.[25] On returning to the project, we took into account the responses that we had received to the CP. We began by considering whether we could continue to support the new structure that the CP had advocated. We concluded that it was not right to do so. We now believe that there are compelling reasons for retaining secondary liability in many cases where P goes on to commit or attempt to commit an offence that D has encouraged or assisted.[26]

---

[20]   Assisting and Encouraging Crime (1993) Law Commission Consultation Paper No 131 ("the CP").

[21]   Para 1.1.

[22]   Para 1.4.

[23]   We set out the Commission's reasons in Part 2 para 2.4 below.

[24]   On which see Part 2 paras 2.2 to 2.3 below.

[25]   We set out the criticism in Part 2 below.

[26]   We set out our reasons in Part 2 below.

1.19   Although we believe that the doctrine of secondary liability should be retained, it is unsatisfactory and in need of reform. In the second of the reports that we are publishing, we will set out our recommendations for a reformed doctrine of secondary liability. In this report we set out our recommendations for a scheme of inchoate liability for encouraging or assisting the commission of offences. We now explain why we are publishing two reports.

TWO REPORTS RATHER THAN ONE

1.20   Originally, we intended to publish a report and draft Bill setting out and explaining a statutory scheme to replace the common law of complicity (including the doctrine of joint venture), incitement and innocent agency.[27] We now believe that it would be better to publish two reports.

1.21   In relation to secondary liability, there is a major issue on which we would like to have the benefit of informed views before we make a final decision. The issue is the correct approach to be adopted (as a matter of policy) to the drafting of new statutory offences to replace the existing common law on secondary liability, particularly against the background of our continuing commitment to codification of the criminal law. The choice for us is, in essence, between two competing approaches.

1.22   The first approach would be to cast the inculpatory provisions imposing secondary liability in quite detailed terms, catering for a variety of circumstances. Adopting this approach would require broad defences to ensure that the Bill did not impose secondary liability where it would be unreasonable to do so. The other approach would be a draft Bill that imposes secondary liability in a more open-textured form, leaving greater scope for judicial development of the principles of liability laid down in the Bill. The provisions imposing secondary liability would, on this approach, be supplemented by a limited number of specific defences and exemptions.

1.23   The issue of the correct approach to the drafting of the Bill as respects secondary liability has greatly exercised us and, indeed, continues to do so. The same issue does not, in our view, arise in relation to the specific new statutory inchoate offences to prohibit the encouragement or assistance of crime. It is for this reason that we feel able to proceed with this report and the draft Bill that accompanies it, before publishing our proposals for reforming the law of secondary liability. In addition, we believe that inchoate liability for encouraging or assisting crime is a matter that merits urgent attention.

1.24   So far as secondary liability is concerned, we have prepared alternative versions of a draft Bill which we have circulated amongst a group of judges, practitioners and academics. Following consideration of their comments and suggestions, we hope to publish a report on secondary liability for encouraging or assisting the commission of offences in the second half of 2006.

---

[27]   Innocent agency is the common law doctrine whereby X is held to have committed an offence as a principal offender if he or she uses another person, who is unaware of the significance of his or her actions, to perpetrate the conduct proscribed by the offence. Thus, X gives a parcel containing a bomb to Y and tells Y to deliver it to V. X tells Y that it is a birthday present for V. As X hoped, the bomb explodes killing V. X is guilty of murder as a principal offender.

AN OUTLINE OF THE RECOMMENDATIONS CONTAINED IN THIS REPORT

The statutory offences that we are recommending[28]

1.25 We are recommending that there should be two new inchoate offences:

(1) encouraging or assisting the commission of an offence ("the principal offence") *intending* to encourage or assist its commission ("the clause 1 offence");

(2) encouraging or assisting the commission of an offence ("the principal offence") *believing* that it will be committed ("the clause 2(1) offence").

Each offence targets very culpable conduct. In order to be convicted of the clause 1 offence, D must not only deliberately seek to encourage or assist P but also do so with the intention that P should commit the principal offence or be encouraged or assisted to commit it. In order to be convicted of the clause 2(1) offence, D must not only deliberately do something capable of encouraging or assisting P but also do so believing that it will encourage or assist P to commit the principal offence and that P will commit the principal offence:

> **Example 1F**
>
> D knows that P wishes to murder V. D, who hates V, provides P with information regarding the whereabouts of V. D's intention is that P should murder V. Meanwhile, Z alerts V to the fact that P intends to kill him. As a result, V goes abroad and P abandons the plan to murder V.

D has committed the clause 1 offence, namely encouraging or assisting murder intending to encourage or assist its commission.

> **Example 1G**
>
> D is a key holder at the office where he works. In return for payment, D makes a copy of the key and gives it to P believing that P will use the key to commit a burglary at the premises. However, D hopes that P will change his mind. P is arrested in connection with another matter before he can even attempt to commit the burglary. P informs the police of what D has done.

In this example, D has committed the clause 2(1) offence because, although not intending that P should commit burglary, D believed that P would commit the offence and that, by giving P a copy of the keys, he would help P to do so.

---

[28] In Part 5 below, we set out and consider in detail the offences that we are recommending.

1.26 The two offences would replace the existing common law offence of incitement and fill the existing gap whereby at common law a person incurs no criminal liability for *assisting* the commission of an offence unless and until the offence is committed or attempted. Each offence may be committed whether or not the principal offence is committed.[29]

Liability for encouraging or assisting more than one principal offence

1.27 Sometimes D may do an act that is capable of encouraging or assisting the commission of more than one principal offence:

> **Example 1H**
>
> In return for payment, D drives P to the house of V. D is not sure whether P will commit burglary, arson or murder. However, D believes that P will commit at least one of those three offences. D drops P near the premises and drives off. P's intention is to commit all three offences but, suspecting that he is being watched, P decides to abandon the project.

D's state of mind is such that, although he or she believes that at least one of three offences will be committed, in relation to each of the three offences the belief is no more than that the offence *might* be committed.

1.28 We are recommending that if D's act is capable of encouraging or assisting the commission of one or more of a number of different principal offences and:

(1) D believes that at least one of them *will* be committed;

(2) D has no belief as to which particular offence will be committed; and

(3) D believes that his or her act will encourage or assist the commission of at least one of those offences,

D may be prosecuted and convicted of encouraging or assisting the commission of any offence that he or she believed might be committed ("the clause 2(2) offence).[30] However, the prosecution will only be able to prosecute D for *one* of the offences that he or she believed might be committed.[31]

---

[29] Clause 3(1) of the draft Bill appended to this report. We consider the implications of this in Part 5 paras 5.8 to 5.9 below.

[30] Clause 2(2) of the draft Bill. In this report, we will use the expression "a clause 2 offence" when referring to both the cl 2(1) offence and the cl 2(2) offence.

[31] Clause 3(4) of the draft Bill. By contrast, D can be prosecuted for and convicted of encouraging or assisting *all* the principal offences that he or she *intended P should commit,* even if he or she believed that P would only commit one of them.

The penalty for each offence

1.29   Subject to one exception, we are recommending that the maximum penalty on conviction of either the clause 1 offence or a clause 2 offence should be the same as if D had been convicted of the principal offence.[32] The exception is where the principal offence is murder. We are recommending that for encouraging or assisting murder, D should be liable to a maximum sentence of life imprisonment rather than the mandatory life sentence.[33]

Defences and Exemptions[34]

1.30   We are recommending that it should be a defence to both the clause 1 and a clause 2 offence if D proves on a balance of probabilities that he or she acted in order to prevent the commission of an offence or the occurrence of harm and that it was reasonable to act as D did:[35]

Example 1J

D is the manager of a public house. P enters the premises with a view to carrying out an assault on a customer, V, because of an unpaid debt. D encourages P instead to take V's briefcase. Before P can take the case, another customer overpowers him.

D has encouraged P to commit theft. However, it might be thought that D ought to be able to say that he or she acted in order to prevent the commission of a more serious offence and that it was reasonable in all the circumstances to encourage P to commit theft. The harm that D was seeking to prevent was greater than any harm resulting from the theft.

1.31   We are also recommending that it should be a defence to a clause 2 offence, but not the clause 1 offence,[36] if D proves on the balance of probabilities that he or she acted reasonably in all the circumstances:[37]

Example 1K

D works as a typist for P. P tells D to type a statement addressed to the solicitors acting for P's wife. D knows that the statement is for the purpose of divorce and ancillary financial relief proceedings that are currently before the county court. In typing the statement, D realises that it contains deliberately misleading information about P's assets.

By typing the letter, D is assisting P to commit an offence. However, it ought to be possible for D to say that he or she acted reasonably because he or she was following her employer's instructions.

---

[32]   Clause 12(1) and (3) of the draft Bill.

[33]   Clause 12(2) of the draft Bill.

[34]   See further Part 6 below.

[35]   Clause 4 of the draft Bill.

[36]   See para 1.32 below.

[37]   Clause 5 of the draft Bill.

1.32   Acting reasonably in all the circumstances would not be a defence to the clause 1 offence. If D intends his or her encouragement or assistance to lead to the commission of an offence, it ought not to be possible for D to have a defence by claiming that what he or she did was within the bounds of reasonableness.

1.33   Our scheme also preserves and refines the common law *Tyrrell*[38] exemption. In *Tyrrell* P, an adult, had unlawful sexual intercourse with D, a child aged between 13 and 16.[39] It was alleged that D had encouraged P to commit the offence. It was held that D could not be convicted of committing the offence as an accessory or of inciting the offence because the offence has been enacted for the purpose of protecting a category of persons and D fell within the category.

1.34   We are recommending that it should be a defence to the clause 1 offence and a clause 2 offence if:

   (1)   the principal offence is one that exists for the protection of a particular category of person;

   (2)   D falls within that category; and

   (3)   D is the victim of the principal offence or would have been had the principal offence been committed.[40]

THE STRUCTURE OF THIS REPORT

1.35   In Part 2 we explain why we are no longer following the proposal in the CP for abolishing the doctrine of secondary liability.

1.36   In Part 3 we provide an outline of the common law.

1.37   In Part 4 we examine the arguments for and against a general inchoate liability for assisting the commission of an offence.

1.38   In Part 5 we explain the new statutory offences that we are recommending.

1.39   In Part 6 we set out and explain the defences that we are recommending.

1.40   In Part 7 we consider the circumstances in which D ought to be inchoately liable for encouraging or assisting P to encourage or assist X to commit an offence.

1.41   In Part 8 we consider extra-territorial jurisdiction in relation to the new offences.

1.42   Part 9 contains a list of recommendations.

---

[38]   [1894] 1 QB 710.

[39]   Contrary to the Criminal Law Amendment Act 1885, s 5.

[40]   Clause 6 of the draft Bill.

1.43   Appendix A explains the provisions of our draft Crime (Encouraging and Assisting) Bill.

1.44   Appendix B examines the liability of a person who assists a suicide that is not subsequently attempted.

PART 2
SHOULD THE DOCTRINE OF SECONDARY LIABILITY BE ABOLISHED?

INTRODUCTION

2.1 In Part 1,[1] we referred to the common law doctrine of secondary liability. Under this doctrine, if D aids, abets, counsels or procures P to commit an offence and P goes on to commit (or attempt to commit) the offence, D is an accessory to and guilty of the offence (or the attempted offence) that P has committed.[2] Accordingly, if P murders V with D's encouragement or assistance, D is guilty of murder and is subject to the mandatory life sentence for murder, just as P is.

2.2 D can aid, abet, counsel or procure P to commit an offence even if there is no agreement between P and D to commit it, for example if D, a trader, sells P an article knowing that P will use it to commit a burglary. Sometimes, however, D and P do agree to commit an offence ("the agreed offence")[3] and subsequently embark on a *joint venture* to commit it. Provided that P commits only the agreed offence, cases of joint venture usually do not pose any particular problems. D is an accessory to the agreed offence because, having agreed with P to commit it, D has aided, abetted, counselled or procured P to commit it.[4]

2.3 However, P may commit an offence ("a collateral offence") which is in addition to or instead of the agreed offence:

> **Example 2A**
>
> D and P agree to commit burglary. In the course of committing it, they are disturbed by the householder, V. Before embarking on the burglary, D, who knew that P was armed with a knife, had urged P to exercise restraint should V disturb them. However, when V disturbs them, P murders V by stabbing V.

The general rule is that D is an accessory to and guilty of a collateral offence if D foresees that P, as an incident of the joint enterprise, *might* commit the offence.[5] If so, it matters not that D was opposed to the commission of the collateral offence. In example 2A, if D foresaw that P might murder V, D is an accessory to and guilty of murder.

---

[1] Para 1.8.

[2] Provided D satisfies the requisite fault element and there is a sufficient connection between D's conduct and P's commission of the offence. D's conduct need not cause P to commit the offence in the sense that, but for D's encouragement or assistance, P would not have committed the offence. However, D's conduct must in fact encourage or assist P to commit the offence. If it does, there is a sufficient connection.

[3] In which case D and P are guilty of conspiracy to commit the agreed offence. An agreement may be inferred from the conduct of D and P.

[4] D, by agreeing with P to commit the agreed offence, is encouraging P to commit it just as P is encouraging D to commit the offence.

[5] *Chan Wing-Siu* [1985] AC 168; *Powell and Daniels* [1999] 1 AC 1.

THE PROPOSALS IN THE CP

2.4 In the CP, the Commission said that the nature of an accessory's liability is essentially inchoate:

> However, the conclusion that an accessory's liability is, *even in the present law*, essentially inchoate in nature springs directly from analysis of the conduct that founds that liability in law. An accessory's legal fault is complete as soon as his act of assistance is done, and acts thereafter by the *principal*, in particular in committing or not committing the crime assisted, cannot therefore add to or detract from that fault. Moreover, it is not the present law, and it is logically impossible that it should become the law, that the accessory must *cause* the commission of the principal crime; and for that reason also the actual occurrence of the principal crime is not taken into account in assessing the accessory's culpability. Even under the present law, therefore, where the principal crime has to be committed before accessory liability can attach, the conditions for the liability of the accessory should be, indeed can only be, assessed at the time of, and in relation to, that act of assistance.[6]

2.5 The Commission proposed that secondary liability for aiding, abetting, counselling or procuring the commission of an offence should be abolished and replaced by two statutory inchoate offences, one of encouraging crime and the other of assisting crime. Therefore, instead of being liable for the offence committed by P, D would be liable for encouraging or assisting its commission. Implicit in the Commission's proposal was a denial that the harm resulting from P's commission of the principal offence should have any legal significance in relation to D's liability.

2.6 However, the Commission canvassed the possibility of retaining the doctrine of joint venture whereby D may be convicted of a collateral offence committed by P in the course of a joint venture.[7] In part, this was because the Commission believed that the ordinary principles underlying secondary liability did not apply in relation to collateral offences. The Commission thought that D, merely by entering into an agreement with P to commit the agreed offence, was not encouraging or assisting P to commit the collateral offence. The Commission, therefore, saw no inconsistency in recommending the abolition of secondary liability for aiding, abetting, counselling or procuring the commission of an offence while possibly retaining some form of accessorial liability for collateral offences committed in the course of a joint venture.[8]

RESPONSES TO THE CP

2.7 Those respondents who provided an analysis of whether inchoate liability should supplant secondary liability focused on:

---

[6] Para 4.24 (emphasis in original).

[7] Paras 4.198 to 4.201 and para 5.2.16.

[8] On this particular issue, Professor Sir John Smith thought that the Commission's position was "frankly baffling" - "Criminal Liability of Accessories: Law and Law Reform" (1997) 113 *Law Quarterly Review* 453, 461.

(1)   forensic considerations,

(2)   public acceptability,

(3)   condemnation and labelling,

(4)   the connection between D's conduct and the offence committed by P.

Forensic considerations

2.8   By virtue of section 8 of the Accessories and Abettors Act 1861, a person who is an accessory can be charged, indicted and punished as a principal offender. This means that the prosecution can obtain a conviction even if it cannot be proved whether the accused was a principal offender or an accessory provided that he or she must have been one or the other.[9] For example, suppose that D1 and D2 are jointly charged with burglary. It is known that one of them entered the premises while the other kept watch. D1 and D2 can each be convicted of burglary despite the prosecution being unable to prove who entered the premises (the principal offender) and who kept watch (the accessory). [10]

2.9   This is of considerable assistance to the prosecution in cases where it is difficult or impossible to prove the precise role of the various parties. In addition, the prosecution does not have to specify in advance whether the allegation is that an accused was a principal offender or an accessory.[11] In *Mercer*[12] it was held that there is no violation of Article 6(3) of the European Convention on Human Rights and Fundamental Freedoms where the prosecution alleges that an accused is a party to an offence but cannot specify his or her precise role.[13]

2.10   Some respondents[14] felt that these forensic advantages would be jeopardised by adopting a scheme consisting solely of inchoate offences. They felt that such a scheme would adversely affect the law's ability to accurately attribute criminal liability in those cases where it is impossible to be sure who was the principal offender and who was the accessory:

---

[9]   *Swindall v Osborne* (1864) 2 Car. & K. 230; *Du Cros v Lambourne* [1907] 1 KB 40; *Ramnath Mohan* [1967] 2 AC 187. D can properly be convicted even if some of the jury find that he or she was the principal offender and some find that he or she was the accessory – *Giannetto* [1997] 1 Cr App R 1 in which the Court of Appeal referred with approval to the decision of the Supreme Court of Canada in *Thatcher v R* (1987) 39 DLR (4th) 275.

[10]   In *Powell and Daniels* [1999] 1 AC 1 it could be proved that the accused was either the person (P) who murdered V or a person (D) who was on a joint venture with P to buy drugs from V believing that P might shoot V with intent to cause serious harm. The accused could be convicted of murder.

[11]   The House of Lords has indicated that it is desirable, wherever possible, for the prosecution to specify whether the accused is alleged to be a principal offender or an accessory – *Maxwell v DPP for Northern Ireland* [1978] 1 WLR 1350.

[12]   [2001] EWCA Crim 638.

[13]   Article 6(3) provides, amongst other things, that everybody charged with a criminal offence has the right "to be informed promptly, in a language which he understands and in detail, of the nature and cause of the accusation against him".

[14]   Professor Sir John Smith, the Crown Prosecution Service and the Society of Public Teachers of Law.

> **Example 2B**
>
> D and P agree to murder V. V is held down and his throat is slit. V dies. The fingerprints of both D and P are on the knife. The prosecution cannot prove whether it was P or D who slit V's throat.

Under the current law, both D and P are guilty of murder. However, under the proposals in the CP, it would be impossible to convict either of murder because it cannot be proved who slit V's throat.

Public acceptability

2.11 Professor Sir John Smith said[15] that the public attaches enormous importance to the consequences that result from a criminal act and that Parliament reacts accordingly. He provided this example:

> **Example 2C**
>
> D gives instructions to P, whom D believes to be a "contract killer" to kill D's partner, V.

Under the proposals in the CP, D would be guilty of the same offence, assisting murder, *irrespective* of whether P decided to kill V or instead to report D to the police.

2.12 Professor Smith doubted whether the public would consider that outcome to be acceptable. He said that society expects an offender to be convicted of and punished for offences that reflect not only his moral culpability but also the harm caused by his or her conduct.[16] Thus, the maximum term of imprisonment for causing dangerous driving is two years[17] but when death is caused the offence becomes causing death by dangerous driving and the maximum term of imprisonment increases to 14 years.[18]

2.13 The Society of Public Teachers of Law[19] agreed. In its view, in a case such as example 2C, should P go on to kill V, it would be unrealistic to attribute responsibility for V's death solely to P given that D would have played a prominent part in bringing about V's death.

---

[15] "Secondary participation in crime – can we do without it?" (1994) 1 *New Law Journal* 679. See also R A Duff, "Acting Trying and Criminal Liability" in S C Shute, J Gardner and J Horder, eds, *Action and Value in Criminal Law* (1993) p 75; Simester and Sullivan, *Criminal Law Theory and Doctrine* (2nd ed 2003) pp 189 to191 and pp 237 to 239.

[16] It is right to acknowledge that not all scholars accept that accurate labelling necessarily requires account to be taken of the harm resulting from conduct – see A J Ashworth, *Principles of Criminal Law* (4th ed 2003) p 91.

[17] Part 1 of sch 2 to the Road Traffic Offenders Act 1988.

[18] Part 1 of sch 2 to the Road Traffic Offenders Act 1988 as amended by the Criminal Justice Act 2003, s 285.

[19] Now the Society of Legal Scholars.

Condemnation, culpability and labelling

2.14 There was criticism that the proposals in the CP would not adequately fulfil the condemnatory and labelling function of the law. In particular, they would not adequately connect an accused with the consequences of his or her offence. According to Professor K J M Smith:

> In the context of complicity, it might be argued that by formally decoupling liability from the commission of the principal harm the complexion of the criminality changes, and along with it part of the justification for punishment. For rather than the existing mental culpability-harm axis of responsibility, criminality would rest substantially on mental culpability only; and, as with inchoate liability generally, there would arguably be a lowering of perceived punishment deserts, alongside a rise in expectations in relation to the appropriate level of mental culpability.[20]

2.15 A specific criticism was that to de-couple an accessory's liability from the harmful consequences of the principal's conduct would be particularly anomalous where the culpability of the former exceeds that of the latter. Professor Sir John Smith provided the following example:

Example 2D

D, a gang leader, sends out his subordinate P to detonate a bomb. P does so without warning in a busy shopping centre. The explosion results in the deaths of 20 people.[21]

2.16 Professor Sir John Smith said[22] that, under the proposals in the CP, P would be liable for 20 murders but D merely for one offence of encouraging murder. The anomaly would be even more striking if D had compelled P to carry out the act by holding P's partner, Z, as a hostage and threatening to kill Z because duress is no defence to murder.[23]

2.17 Sometimes, death is an unexpected and unforeseen consequence:

Example 2E

D encourages P to inflict grievous bodily harm on V. P does so. Normally V's injuries would not prove fatal. However, medical complications set in and V dies.

Under the current law, both D and P are guilty of murder. Under the proposals in the CP, P would be guilty of murder but D would be guilty only of encouraging P to cause grievous bodily harm with intent.

---

[20] "The Law Commission Consultation Paper on Complicity: (1) A Blueprint for Rationalism" [1994] *Criminal Law Review* 239, 244.

[21] "Criminal Liability of Accessories: Law and Law Reform" (1997) 113 *Law Quarterly Review* 453, 460.

[22] Above.

[23] *Howe* [1987] AC 417.

2.18 Professor Sir John Smith agreed that it is arguable that in example 1E neither D nor P should be held responsible for the unintended and unforeseen consequences. However, the proposals in the CP lead to a conclusion that he thought even less acceptable, namely that P is held responsible for those consequences whereas D, the more culpable party, is not held responsible.

The connection between D's conduct and P's offence

2.19 In the CP, the Commission said that D's liability for encouraging or assisting P to commit an offence should be inchoate because it was impossible to connect D to P's offence. Professor K J M Smith questioned this assertion:

> … it has always been implied in the concept of complicity that an accessory's involvement … did make some difference to the outcome, and, as a consequence of this, accessories have been implicitly linked to the harm element in the principal offence. No other plausible explanation exists for complicity's tenacious, fundamental requirement of the commission of the principal offence. … . In sum then, under existing doctrine, the accessory's liability is derivative or parasitic of a principal offence and its harm content. Rather than relying solely on the accessory's mental culpability, unlike inchoate liability, complicity responsibility also implicitly draws on the attributable harm of the principal offence.[24]

CONCLUSION

2.20 We acknowledge that it is possible to preserve some of the forensic benefits of the current law in a scheme consisting solely of inchoate offences. This could be achieved by a statutory provision stating that if the prosecution can prove that D must have been either the principal offender or the encourager/assister, D can be convicted of the inchoate offence.[25]

2.21 However, such a provision would not meet the criticism that the proposals in the CP would not accurately label and condemn D for his or her conduct:

Example 2F

D gives P chocolates to give to V. V eats them and dies because they are poisoned. D knew the chocolates were poisoned and would kill anyone who ate them.

Under the proposals in the CP, D would be guilty of murder if P was unaware that the chocolates were poisoned because P would be an innocent agent and D would be considered to have perpetrated the offence as a principal offender. However, if P knew that the chocolates were poisoned, P would be guilty of murder but D would be guilty of assisting murder.

---

[24] "The Law Commission Consultation Paper on Complicity: (1) A Blueprint for Rationalism" [1994] *Criminal Law Review* 239, 244.

[25] See cl 10 of the draft Bill.

2.22   Example 2F illustrates why it would be wrong to abolish secondary liability. It cannot be right that D is guilty of murder if P is unaware that the chocolates are poisoned but only of assisting murder if P is aware that the chocolates are poisoned. D's conduct and state of mind are identical in each case. Further, whereas examples 2D and 2E might be thought to reveal problems with specific aspects of the law of murder that might be better resolved by reforming those aspects, the anomaly in example 2F is not the product of any defects in the law of murder.

2.23   We believe that if P commits an offence that it was D's intention P should commit,[26] account should be taken of D's connection with the harm that results from P committing the offence. D's state of mind in intending that the offence should be committed connects D to the offence and the resulting harm in a morally significant way that can only be properly reflected by convicting D of the offence rather than encouraging or assisting the commission of the offence. In as much as there is a difference in the culpability of P and D, this can be reflected in the nature or severity of the punishment each is to receive for his or her involvement.[27]

2.24   Further, we also believe that if P in the course of a joint venture commits a collateral offence that D foresaw that P might commit, account should be taken of D's connection with the harm that results from P committing the offence. It is true that D does not intend that P should commit the collateral offence and may even be opposed to the commission of the offence. However, D, by participating in the joint venture, contributes to the circumstances giving rise to the commission of the collateral offence. Further, by contemplating the collateral offence as a possible incident of the unlawful venture and nevertheless deciding to participate, D consciously accepts the risk that such an offence might be committed.[28]

2.25   We acknowledge that the retention of secondary liability may sometimes result in D being liable for unexpected consequences. However, this will usually be the result of anomalies in the substantive law that the doctrine of secondary liability must accommodate. The doctrine of secondary liability is of general application, applying to many different offences whether or not those offences are well structured, well defined or even consistent with one another. Removing D's, but not P's, liability for unforeseen consequences, would simply create a new anomaly.

---

[26]   This would include an agreed offence committed in the course of a joint venture.

[27]   Although comparisons can be misleading, it is at least noteworthy that in the United States of America, in a study of multi-party death penalty cases, it was found that in 63.6% of cases the principals were executed but not the accessories. By way of contrast, only in 32.3% of cases were both the principals and the accessories executed and in a mere 4.1% of cases were the accessories executed but not the principals: Joshua Dressler, "The Jurisprudence of Death by Another: Accessories and Capital Punishment" (1979) *University of Colorado Law Review* 17, 69.

[28]   In the second of our reports, we will be setting out and explaining our proposals for secondary liability, including explaining why we believe that holding D secondarily liable for a collateral offence committed in the course of a joint venture is justified in principle and as a matter of policy.

2.26 One aim of the proposals in the CP was to simplify the law by creating a clear distinction between the liability of the principal offender and the liability of the accessory. We now believe that this simplicity comes at too high a price. If P commits an offence that D either intended should be committed or believed might be committed in the course of a joint venture, there are compelling reasons for convicting D of the offence should P commit it. We now believe that to confine D's liability in such cases to that of encouraging or assisting the offence would be to confine it too narrowly.

PART 3
AN OUTLINE OF THE PRESENT LAW OF INCHOATE LIABILITY FOR ENCOURAGING OR ASSISTING CRIME

INTRODUCTION

3.1 In this Part we provide an outline of the common law of inchoate liability for encouraging or assisting the commission of an offence. We begin by focusing on what we consider to be its main defect.

A SERIOUS GAP IN THE COMMON LAW

3.2 At common law if P commits or attempts to commit an offence, it matters not whether D encouraged, on the one hand, or assisted, on the other, P to commit the offence. D is an accessory to and guilty of the offence (or the attempt to commit it) provided that the encouragement or assistance in fact contributed to the commission of the offence. However, what if D's encouragement or assistance fails to bear fruit? This could be because:

  (1)   P does not commit or attempt to commit the offence:

Example 3A

D, knowing that P is intending to burgle V's premises, leaves a ladder outside V's house in order to assist P to enter the premises. On learning that V has returned from holiday earlier than expected, P abandons the project.

---

  (2)   P does commit or attempt to commit the offence but without reference to the assistance or encouragement that D has provided:

Example 3B

D, knowing that P intends to burgle V's premises, leaves a ladder outside V's house to assist P to enter the premises. P, unaware that D has left the ladder, commits the burglary without using the ladder.

---

  (3)   P commits or attempts to commit the offence but without recourse to or reliance on D's assistance or encouragement because D has not provided it by the time P commits or attempts to commit the offence:

Example 3C

D sends a cheque in the post to P who has appealed for funds to enable him to publish and distribute an abusive and insulting pamphlet intended to stir up racial hatred. The cheque does not arrive but P is still able to publish the leaflet.

At common law, D is not criminally liable in any of the three examples despite having done his or her best to assist P to commit an offence.

3.3   In examples 3B and 3C, it might be thought that D, by virtue of trying to assist P, could be convicted of *attempting* to commit the offence that P has committed.[1] However, it is not an offence to attempt to aid, abet, counsel, procure or suborn the commission of an offence.[2] That leaves the possibility of D being inchoately liable for assisting P to commit an offence. However, the common law does not recognise inchoate liability for assisting the commission of an offence if the offence is not subsequently committed or is committed without reference to D's assistance.

3.4   In examples 3A to 3C, instead of seeking to render assistance, D might have sought to render *encouragement* by urging D to commit burglary or by posting a letter encouraging P to publish the racist pamphlet. Had D done so, in examples 3A and 3B, he or she would have been guilty of the common law inchoate offence of incitement. In example 3C, D would have been guilty of attempting to incite.[3]

3.5   The difference in the way that the common law treats encouragement and assistance for the purposes of inchoate liability is striking. There is a possible historical explanation. In developing the inchoate offences, the courts sought to identify a cogent reason to justify imposing criminal liability for conduct that merely enhanced the prospect of actual harm occurring. The cogent reason that they identified was an *intention* on the part of D to bring about harm. Although there will be exceptions, those who encourage others to commit an offence generally do so with the intention that the offence be committed. The same is not true of those who render assistance. Such persons, particularly if the assistance is rendered in return for payment, are frequently indifferent as to whether or not the offence is committed.

3.6   Whatever the explanation, the rendering of assistance, no less than the rendering of encouragement, increases the likelihood of harm occurring. The Supreme Court of Canada, identifying the rationale underlying liability for incitement, has recently observed:

---

[1]   By contrast, in example 3A, it would be absurd if D, although having done all that he or she set out to do, could be an accessory to attempted burglary in circumstances where P has not attempted to commit the offence – see J C Smith, "Secondary participation and inchoate offences" in C F H Tapper (ed) *Crime, Proof & Punishment, Essays in Honour of Sir Rupert Cross* (1981) 21, 37.

[2]   Criminal Attempts Act 1981, s 1(4)(b). The wording of the provision is based on a fallacy, namely that "aiding, abetting counselling, procuring or suborning" an offence is an offence known to English law. There is no such offence. A person who aids, abets counsels or procures the commission of an offence is guilty of the offence that he or she has aided, abetted, counselled or procured. As interpreted in *Dunnington* [1984] QB 472, the provision does not prevent D being convicted of attempt where his or her conduct does in fact encourage or assist P but P's attempt to commit the principal offence is unsuccessful. In such a case, both D and P are guilty of attempt to commit the principal offence. However, it does prevent D being convicted of attempting to commit an offence *that has been committed by P* if, despite trying to encourage or assist P, D's conduct does not in fact do so, as in examples 3B and 3C above.

[3]   *Banks and Banks* (1873) 12 Cox CC 393; *Ransford* (1874) 13 Cox CC 9; *R v Chelmsford Justices, ex p Amos* [1973] *Criminal Law Review* 437.

... if the primary act (for example, killing) is harmful, society will want people not to do it. Equally, it will not want them even to try to do it, or to counsel or incite others to do it. For while the act itself causes actual harm, attempting to do it, or counselling, inciting or procuring someone else to do it, are sources of potential harm − they increase the likelihood of that particular harm's occurrence.[4]

The rationale applies with equal force to acts of assistance.

3.7 Partly because of the absence at common law of an inchoate offence of assisting crime, Parliament has enacted a considerable number of statutory offences that criminalise particular instances of inchoate assistance.[5] However, there are no statutory inchoate offences of assisting some of the most serious, including murder, robbery, blackmail or burglary. We agree with Professor John Spencer that there "is a general problem, and it needs a general solution".[6]

3.8 In addition, Professor Spencer has argued that the lack of a general inchoate offence of assisting crime has had an unfortunate knock-on effect, which we now consider.

THE DISTORTION OF OTHER OFFENCES TO COMPENSATE FOR THE LACK OF INCHOATE LIABILITY FOR ASSISTING CRIME

3.9 According to Professor Spencer:

... the lack of an inchoate offence of facilitation creates a theoretical gap in the criminal law through which undeserving rogues threaten to escape, and [which] the courts regularly plug ... by bending other offences, with baleful side effects.[7]

The offences to which he was referring to include statutory conspiracy and common law conspiracy to defraud.

Statutory conspiracy

3.10 Section 1(1) of the Criminal Law Act 1977 provides:

[I]f a person agrees with any other person or persons that a course of conduct shall be pursued which, if the agreement is carried out in accordance with their intentions, ... will necessarily amount to or involve the commission of any offence ... by one or more of the parties to the agreement ... he is guilty of conspiracy to commit the offence ... in question.

---

4 *R v Hamilton* 2005 SCC 47, para 25, by Fish J delivering the judgement of the majority of the Supreme Court of Canada.

5 Examples are Treason Act 1351; Prison Act 1952, s 39; Forgery and Counterfeiting Act 1981, s 17(1); Computer Misuse Act 1990, s 2(1)(b) and 2(3); Terrorism Act 2000, ss 12(2) and 17; Asylum and Immigration (Treatment of Claimants, etc) Act 2004, s 4(2).

6 "Trying to help another person commit a crime" in P Smith (ed) *Essays in Honour of J C Smith* (1987) 148, 159.

7 Above, 148 to 149.

3.11   Prior to the enactment of s 1(1), the Law Commission had recommended that "the law should require full intention and knowledge before a conspiracy can be established".[8] The reference to "full intention" denoted an intention to bring about any consequence specified in the definition of the actus reus of the substantive offence.[9] During the Criminal Law Bill's passage through Parliament, the Lord Chancellor stated that "the law should require full intention and knowledge before conspiracy can be established".[10] It seems therefore that Parliament intended that a party to an agreement should be guilty of statutory conspiracy only if he or she intended that the agreed offence should be committed.

3.12   In *Anderson*[11] D, in return for payment, agreed with P that he would help P escape from prison by providing some cutting equipment. No attempt was made to put the plan into effect. D was charged with conspiracy to effect the escape of a prisoner.[12] D submitted that he could not be convicted of the offence because, although he had intended to provide the equipment, he had never intended that the escape plan should be carried into effect. Additionally, he claimed that he believed that the escape plan could not possibly succeed. After an adverse indication by the trial judge, D pleaded guilty.

3.13   The House of Lords upheld D's conviction. It was sufficient to prove that, when entering into the agreement, D knew that the envisaged course of action, *if pursued*, would involve the commission of an offence and that he had intended to play some part in the agreed course of conduct. Lord Bridge articulated the policy reasons underlying the decision:

> I am clearly driven by the diversity of roles which parties may agree to play in criminal conspiracies to reject any construction of the statutory language which would require the prosecution to prove an intent on the part of each conspirator that the criminal offence … should in fact … be committed. A simple example will illustrate the absurdity to which this construction would lead. The proprietor of a car firm agrees for a substantial payment to make available a hire car to a gang for use in a robbery … . Being fully aware of the circumstances of the robbery in which the car is proposed to be used he is plainly a party to the conspiracy to rob.… . Yet, once he has been paid, it will be a matter of complete indifference to him whether the robbery is in fact committed or not. … Parliament cannot have intended that such parties should escape conviction of conspiracy on the basis that it cannot be proved against them that they intended that the relevant offence or offences should be committed.[13]

---

[8]   Report on Conspiracy and Criminal Law Reform (1976) Law Com No 76 at para 1.39.

[9]   Above, para 7.2(5).

[10]   Hansard (HL) 20 January 1977, vol 379, cols 154-155.

[11]   [1986] AC 27.

[12]   Contrary to the Criminal Law Act 1977, s 1(1).

[13]   [1986] AC 27, 38.

The effect of the decision is that there can be a criminal conspiracy which none of the conspirators intend to carry out.[14]

3.14 It is true that, even if there had been an inchoate offence of assisting crime, there would still have been a need in *Anderson* to distort the law of conspiracy in order to secure D's conviction. This is because D was injured in a traffic accident before he could provide or attempt to provide the cutting equipment and he, therefore, did not provide any assistance. However, an inchoate offence of assisting crime would address the policy concerns expressed by Lord Bridge in cases where D *does* provide assistance pursuant to the agreement that he or she enters into.

Conspiracy to defraud

3.15 In *Hollinshead*[15] the accused - D1, D2 and D3 – manufactured and agreed to sell to X, an under-cover police officer, devices to be fitted to electricity meters to make them under-record the amount of electricity used. They expected X to re-sell the devices to users of electricity for use in defrauding electricity boards. They were charged with conspiring to aid, abet, counsel or procure persons unknown to commit the offence of evading liability by deception[16] and, alternatively, with conspiracy to defraud. They were convicted of conspiracy to defraud.

3.16 The House of Lords held that they had been rightly convicted of conspiracy to defraud because they manufactured and sold the devices for the dishonest purpose of enabling the devices to be used to the detriment of electricity boards. The decision is open to two objections. First, the purpose of the accused was to make a profit rather than to cause loss to electricity boards. This was unaffected by the fact that the only function of the devices was to cause loss to electricity boards. Secondly, the conspiracy did not involve any of the accused perpetrating the contemplated fraud. The accused had merely conspired to manufacture and sell the devices. In executing their conspiracy and selling the devices, they were not defrauding anyone.

---

[14] Subsequent cases have shown a reluctance to follow *Anderson*. In *McPhillips* [1989] NI 360 the Court of Appeal of Northern Ireland sought to distinguish it. In *Yip-Chiu-Cheung* [1995] 1 AC 111, a case of common law conspiracy, the Privy Council, without referring to *Anderson*, held that the prosecution must prove that each conspirator intends the agreement to be carried out. In *Edwards* [1991] *Criminal Law Review* 45 the Court of Appeal held that D was guilty of conspiracy to supply amphetamine only if he intended to supply it. However, again the Court made no reference to *Anderson*. More recently, Lord Nicholls, without referring to *Anderson*, said, "The conspirators must intend to do the act prohibited by the substantive offence" – *Saik* [2006] UKHL; [2006] 2 WLR 993.

[15] [1985] AC 975.

[16] Contrary to the Theft Act 1978, s 2.

3.17 The decision makes it possible to convict of conspiracy to defraud those who contemplate that the execution of their agreement will facilitate a third party to perpetrate a fraud. According to Professor Spencer, the House of Lords did so by making "an offence which was already vague and amorphous even more so".[17] The need to do so would have been obviated had there been an inchoate offence of assisting crime.

THE COMMON LAW OFFENCE OF INCITEMENT

Introduction

3.18 The common law inchoate offence of incitement imposes criminal liability in respect of conduct by D that *encourages* P to commit an offence. Provided D satisfies the fault element of the offence, D is liable as soon as the encouragement comes to P's attention. If P is in fact encouraged and does commit the offence, D is guilty of the offence as an accessory.

The elements of the offence

The proscribed conduct

3.19 It is clear that to propose, to persuade or to exhort another person to commit an offence is to engage in the proscribed conduct of the offence. In *Marlow*[18] the Court of Appeal referred to "encourage" and said that the word "represents as well as any word can the concept involved".[19] *Marlow* confirms that there does not have to be an element of persuasion or pressure.

3.20 The incitement may be implied. In *Invicta Plastics Ltd v Clare*,[20] D was convicted of incitement by virtue of advertising a device that could not be used without at the same time committing the offence that D was charged with inciting. In contrast, a mere intention to manufacture and sell a device that cannot be used without committing an offence does not amount to incitement.[21]

---

[17] "Trying to help another person commit an offence" in P Smith (ed) *Essays in Honour of J C Smith* (1987) 148, 156.

[18] [1997] *Criminal Law Review* 897 in which D published a book that contained advice on the cultivation of cannabis. By contrast, in A Criminal Code for England and Wales vol 2 Commentary on Draft Criminal Code Bill (1989) Law Com No 177, the Commission specifically rejected (para 13.6) the suggestion that "encourage" rather than "incite" should be used to describe the conduct component. It was feared that "encourage" might be interpreted as requiring that the person incited was actually encouraged.

[19] Above.

[20] [1976] RTR 251. In "Trying to help another person commit a crime" P Smith (ed) *Essays in Honour of JC Smith* (1987) 148, 152 to 154, Professor Spencer has criticised the decision and cites it as another illustration of how the lack at common law of inchoate liability for assisting the commission of an offence has led to the distortion of other offences.

[21] *James and Ashford* (1985) 82 Cr App R 226, 232.

3.21   The conduct element is capable of being satisfied even if the initiative is taken by P in the form of inviting D to encourage P to commit an offence. In *Goldman*[22] P published an advertisement inviting readers to buy indecent photographs of children under 16. D replied offering to buy the photographs. D was convicted of attempting to incite P to distribute indecent photographs of children under 16.[23]

3.22   The target of D's incitement has to be a person[24] but it does not have to be a particular individual or group. In *Most*[25] D was held liable for inciting murder on the basis of a newspaper article he wrote seemingly addressed to the world in which he encouraged political assassinations.[26]

3.23   The encouragement must come to the attention of the intended recipient[27] but it is not necessary that anyone is in fact encouraged.[28] Thus, in *Marlow*[29] D would have been liable even if nobody reading his book had been encouraged to cultivate cannabis. Likewise, in *DPP v Armstrong*[30] D was liable for inciting an undercover police officer to distribute indecent photographs of children under 16 despite the officer himself never having any intention of distributing the material.

---

[22]   [2001] *Criminal Law Review* 894.

[23]   It is unclear why D was charged with attempting to incite rather than incitement. Simester and Sullivan, *Criminal Law Theory and Doctrine* (2ⁿᵈ ed 2003) p 265 criticises the decision on the grounds that it extends the natural meaning of incitement and, thereby, enables the willing purchaser of a controlled drug to be convicted of inciting the supplier to commit the offence of supplying a controlled drug.

[24]   It is not an offence to incite a machine. It is true that in *O'Shea* [2004] *Criminal Law Review* 894 the Court of Appeal accepted that, by subscribing to a website with indecent images of children, there was a prima facie case that D had incited P, the business offering supply on the site, even though D's communication had been with a wholly automated computer system. However, as Smith and Hogan, *Criminal Law* (11ᵗʰ ed 2005) p 352 points out, "... D's communication with [P] can be proved from evidence that the business responded for example, by producing bi-weekly updates to the website to reflect requests".

[25]   (1881) 7 QBD 244.

[26]   In *Invicta Plastics Ltd v Clare* [1976] RTR 251 D was held liable for inciting motorists generally.

[27]   *Banks and Banks* (1873) 12 Cox CC 393; *Ransford* (1874) 13 Cox CC 9. If the target of the incitement is a group of persons, it suffices if the encouragement comes to the attention of one of them. If the target is people generally, it must come to the attention of someone.

[28]   *Most* (1881) 7 QBD 244; *DPP v Armstrong* [2000] *Criminal Law Review* 379.

[29]   [1997] *Criminal Law Review* 897.

[30]   [2000] *Criminal Law Review* 379.

3.24   If the encouragement does not come to P's attention, D can be convicted of attempting to incite[31] provided that the offence incited is triable on indictment or triable either way[32] and D does an act that is more than merely preparatory to the commission of the full offence.[33] Thus, if D posts a letter to P urging P to murder V but the letter is intercepted or reaches but is never read by P, D is guilty of attempt to incite murder.

The conduct incited

3.25   The general principle is that the act incited must be one that, if done, would involve P committing a substantive offence[34] as a principal offender. The principle gives rise to problems in cases where, were the act incited to be done:

(1)   P would not commit any offence;

(2)   P would commit an inchoate, but not a substantive, offence;

(3)   P would commit a substantive offence but as an accessory rather than a principal offender.

INCITING P TO DO AN ACT WHICH, IF DONE, WOULD NOT INVOLVE P COMMITTING ANY OFFENCE

P is aged under 10

3.26   There is a conclusive presumption that a child under 10 cannot be guilty of a criminal offence.[35] If P encourages a child under 10 to commit an offence, whether or not D is criminally liable may depend on whether or not the child commits or attempts to commit the offence. If the child does commit or attempt to commit the offence, D, by virtue of the doctrine of innocent agency, is guilty of the offence that he or she has encouraged the child to commit.[36]

3.27   However, there is no authority that has applied the doctrine of innocent agency to incitement. It is uncertain, therefore, whether D can be guilty of incitement if he or she encourages a child under 10 to commit an offence if the child, for whatever reason, does not commit or attempt to commit the offence.

---

[31]   *Banks and Banks* (1873) 12 Cox CC; *Ransford* (1874) 13 Cox CC 9; *R v Chelmsford Justices ex p Amos* [1973] *Criminal Law Review* 437. Whereas, the Criminal Attempts Act 1981 abolished the offence of attempt to commit conspiracy it left intact attempt to incite.

[32]   Criminal Attempts Act 1981, s 1(4).

[33]   Criminal Attempts Act 1981, s 1(1).

[34]   As opposed to an inchoate offence.

[35]   Children and Young Persons Act 1933, s 50.

[36]   See Part 1 n 27 above.

The offence cannot be committed by P because it exists for P's protection[37]

3.28 In *Tyrrell*[38] D, a girl aged between 13 and 16 encouraged P to have sexual intercourse with her. It was an offence for a man to have sexual intercourse with a child aged between 13 and 16.[39] D was charged with being an accessory to P's offence and, alternatively, with inciting P to commit the offence. Lord Coleridge CJ said that the Criminal Law Amendment Act 1885 had been passed "for the purpose of protecting women and children against themselves"[40]. He concluded that it was impossible to say that Parliament intended that those persons for whose protection an offence had been created could be convicted of being an accessory to the offence or of inciting it.[41]

3.29 Subsequently, the Court of Appeal has held that if D incites P to commit an offence that P cannot commit because of the *Tyrrell* exemption, D cannot be guilty of inciting P to commit the offence.[42] In doing so, the Court of Appeal decided that it was not an offence at common law for a man to incite a girl of 15 to permit him to have sexual intercourse with her. Lord Justice Scarman said that the Court had reached its decision with regret and that "plainly a gap or lacuna in the protection of girls under the age of 16 is exposed by [the court's decision]".[43] The decision enables D to take advantage of a principle designed for the protection of P.[44]

P does not satisfy the fault element of the offence

3.30 In some cases, were P to perpetrate the act incited, P would lack the fault element of the offence:

Example 3D

D encourages P to have sexual intercourse with V. D tells P to ignore any protest by V because V enjoys feigning lack of consent even when she is consenting. D knows that what he is telling P is untrue.

---

[37] For detailed discussion, see Professor Glanville Williams, "Victims and other exempt parties in crime" (1990) 10 *Legal Studies* 245.

[38] [1894] 1QB 710.

[39] Criminal Law Amendment Act 1885, s 5.

[40] [1894] 1 QB 710, 712.

[41] At least if the protected person is or would be the *victim* of the principal offence.

[42] *Whitehouse* [1977] QB 868. See also *Pickford* [1995] 1 Cr App R 420, 424. In response to the decision in *Whitehouse*, the Criminal Law Act 1977, s 54 made it an offence to incite a girl under 16 to have incestuous sexual intercourse but the general principle is unaffected.

[43] [1977] QB 868, 875.

[44] The Court of Appeal has recently applied *Whitehouse* in the context of incitement to commit buggery – *Claydon* [2005] EWCA Crim 2827; [2006] 1 Cr App R 20. The Court said that it too reached its decision with regret.

If P had intercourse with (non-consenting) V but under a reasonable belief that she was consenting, P would not be guilty of rape.[45] There is authority, however, that in those circumstances D would be guilty of rape as an accessory despite the fact that P has not committed the offence.[46] Yet, it seems that if P decides not to have intercourse with V, D cannot be convicted of incitement to rape. This is because the Court of Appeal has held that in order for D to be guilty of incitement, P must satisfy the fault element of the principal offence.[47]

P acting under duress

3.31 Duress is a complete defence to all offences except murder,[48] attempted murder[49] and, possibly, some forms of treason. The defence does not negate the fault element of the offence and, therefore, if P successfully pleads the defence he or she is acquitted despite having satisfied all the elements of the offence:

Example 3E

D encourages P to rape V and threatens P with serious harm if he does not do so. Fortunately, the police arrive before the intercourse occurs.

It is clear that had P had intercourse with non-consenting V, P would have been able to plead duress as a complete defence to a charge of rape. It is also clear that, as in example 3D, D would be guilty of the offence as an accessory despite the fact that P not committed the offence.[50] However, there is no authority on whether D can be convicted of incitement if P does not have intercourse with V because, for example, of the fortuitous intervention of a third party.

3.32 We acknowledge that the fact that, in examples 3D and 3E, D can be convicted of being an accessory should P commit the act incited, is not a conclusive reason why D should be guilty of incitement if P does not perpetrate the act. As Smith and Hogan points out, in cases of incitement "the full offence is merely in prospect".[51] Nevertheless, we believe that it is unsatisfactory for D to incur no criminal liability in circumstances where the reason that P would not commit an offence is D's own reprehensible conduct.

INCITING P TO COMMIT AN INCHOATE OFFENCE

3.33 Cases of incitement usually involve D encouraging P to commit a substantive offence. Sometimes, however, D incites P to commit an inchoate offence:

(1) D incites P to incite X to assault V; or

(2) D incites P1 and P2 to conspire to assault V.

---

[45] Sexual Offences Act 2003, s 1(1)(c).

[46] *Cogan and Leak* [1976] QB 217.

[47] *Curr* [1968] 2 QB 944. In paras 3.46 to 3.48 we consider *Curr* in more detail

[48] *Howe* [1987] AC 417

[49] *Gotts* [1992] 2 AC 412

[50] *Bourne* (1952) 36 Cr App R 125.

[51] *Criminal Law* (11th ed 2005) p 356.

3.34   The inchoate offences of incitement, conspiracy and attempt punish conduct that is a step removed from the commission of the principal offence. However, in cases where D incites P to incite X to assault V, D's conduct is two steps removed from the principal offence. The underlying problem is in identifying the point at which conduct is so far removed from the commission of a principal offence that it ought not to be criminalised.[52]

Incitement to commit conspiracy

3.35   At common law it was an offence for D to incite P1 and P2 to conspire to commit an offence:

Example 3F

D, who hates V, encourages P1 and P2 to agree to murder V.

If P1 and P2 reach agreement, P1 and P2 are guilty of conspiracy to murder and, D, by encouraging them, is also guilty of the offence as an accessory. However, should P1 and P2 fail to reach agreement, D is not criminally liable because in 1977 Parliament abolished the common law offence of incitement to commit conspiracy.[53]

Incitement to commit incitement

3.36   By contrast, D can be convicted of inciting P to incite X to commit an offence:

Example 3G

D urges P to encourage X to murder V. Instead, P reports D to the police. `

D is guilty of inciting P to incite X to commit murder.[54]

3.37   However, recognising that Parliament had abolished the offence of incitement to commit conspiracy, the Court of Appeal has said that a charge of incitement to incite does not lie if the incitement takes the form of inciting P to enter into a conspiracy with a third party.[55] This led the Law Commission to observe, "In relation to incitement the present law has reached the point of absurdity".[56]

Incitement to commit attempt

3.38   It must be unusual for a person to incite another to commit an attempt rather than the completed offence. However, it is possible to envisage an example:

---

[52]   We consider this issue in detail in Part 7.

[53]   Criminal Law Act 1977, s 5(7). However, Parliament has not abolished the common law offence of conspiracy to incite so that D and P can be convicted of, for example, conspiring to incite X to murder V – *Booth* [1999] *Criminal Law Review* 144.

[54]   *Sirat* (1985) 83 Cr App R 41; *Evans* [1986] *Criminal Law Review* 470.

[55]   *Sirat* (1985) 83 Cr App R 41.

[56]   Criminal Law: A Criminal Code for England and Wales, vol 2 Commentary on Draft Criminal Code Bill (1989) Law Com No 177, para 13.13,

> **Example 3H**
>
> D, a drug dealer, has previously supplied V with heroin for which V has failed to pay. V requests a further supply. D agrees but, to teach V a lesson, decides to supply V with an innocuous substance. D tells one of his "runners", P, to take the substance to V. D tells P that the substance is heroin. P is arrested before he can take the substance to V. P informs the police of what D had asked him to do.

The defence of impossibility has been abolished for the statutory offence of attempt.[57] Therefore, had P supplied the substance to X, P would have been guilty of attempting to supply a controlled drug to another person.[58] Accordingly, although there is no direct authority, in principle D ought to be guilty of inciting P to attempt to supply a controlled drug.[59]

INCITING P TO COMMIT AN OFFENCE AS AN ACCESSORY

3.39   It is uncertain whether it is an offence to incite a person to commit an offence as an accessory:

> **Example 3J**
>
> D encourages P to encourage X to rob V. P is arrested before being able to encourage X.

There is no doubt that D has committed the offence of inciting P to incite X to commit robbery.[60] The issue is whether D can be convicted of inciting P to commit robbery.

3.40   In *Whitehouse*[61] the Court of Appeal appears to have assumed that an offence of inciting another to commit an offence as an accessory is an offence known to English law. The facts were that D incited his daughter to commit incest with him. In fact, no sexual intercourse took place and there was no attempt at sexual intercourse. Under what was section 11 of the Sexual Offences Act 1956, a girl under the age of 16 could not be guilty of incest. The prosecution, in seeking to uphold D's conviction, submitted that, although D could not be guilty of inciting his daughter to commit incest as a principal offender, he could be guilty of inciting his daughter to be an accessory to incest.

---

[57]   Criminal Attempts Act, s 1(3).

[58]   Contrary to the Criminal Attempts Act 1981, s 1(1). D would have been an accessory to P's attempt – *Hapgood and Wyatt* (1870) LR1 CCR 221.

[59]   In passing, it should be noted that X, by asking D to supply cannabis, has incited P to supply a controlled drug.

[60]   See para 3.36 above.

[61]   [1977] QB 868.

3.41   If inciting another to commit an offence as an accessory is not an offence known to English law, the Court of Appeal could have quashed D's conviction on that short ground. Instead, the Court allowed D's appeal on a different ground, namely that the act incited must be one that, when done, would be a crime by the person incited.[62] D could not be guilty of inciting his daughter to be an accessory to the offence because, had intercourse been attempted or taken place, she would not have been an accessory to her father's offence because of the *Tyrrell* exemption.[63]

3.42   However, a subsequent ruling suggests that incitement to commit an offence as an accessory is not an offence known to English law. In *Bodin*,[64] D arranged with P that P would find a third party, X, to assault V. In the event, P did nothing and the assault never took place. D was charged with inciting P to assault V. Had the assault taken place, P would have been guilty of the offence not as a principal offender but as an accessory. The trial judge ruled that the conduct that D incites must involve P committing an offence as a principal offender and not as an accessory. If *Bodin* is an accurate statement of the law, in example 3K D is guilty of inciting P to incite X to commit robbery but not of inciting robbery.

3.43   The view of leading commentators[65] is that the law is as stated in *Bodin*. Commenting on the case, Simester and Sullivan state:

> Perhaps what lies behind the ruling in *Bodin* is the idea that acts of complicity are too remote from the commission of the principal offence to fall within the mischief of incitement. If this is the reason, it does not sit well with the fact that it is quite irrelevant to liability for incitement whether or not the principal offence is committed.[66]

The fault element of incitement

Introduction

3.44   According to Smith and Hogan:

---

[62]   See para 3.29 above.

[63]   *Tyrrell* [1894] 1 QB 710 – see para 3.28 above. The daughter in *Whitehouse* was a member of the class of persons that the offence in question was designed to protect.

[64]   [1979] *Criminal Law Review* 176. Since it is a Crown Court ruling it is of no formal authority. However, it was referred to without criticism by the Court of Appeal in *Sirat* (1985) 83 Cr App R 41.

[65]   Smith and Hogan, *Criminal Law* (11th ed 2005) p 357; Simester and Sullivan, *Criminal Law Theory and Doctrine* (2nd ed 2003) p 266.

[66]   *Criminal Law Theory and Doctrine* (2nd ed 2003) p 266.

The mens rea of incitement is crucial to the offence and has given rise to confusion in the courts resulting in an unfortunate lack of clarity in the law. It comprises two elements. First, as with attempts, D must intend the consequences specified in the actus reus. ... . The second element ... is that, as in the case of counselling and abetting, the prosecution must prove that D knew of (or deliberately closed his eyes to) all the circumstances of the act incited which are elements of the crime in question.[67]

D's attitude towards the commission of the act incited

3.45 There is no definitive analysis in the case law of what D's attitude towards the commission of the principal offence must be. The authorities point to two possibilities. One leading case suggests that it must be D's purpose that P should commit the principal offence or at least that P should be encouraged to commit it.[68] A requirement of purpose would be consistent with the origin of incitement as a species of attempt.[69] The same case, however, can be interpreted as authority for the proposition that it suffices if D believes that, were P to act on the encouragement, P would inevitably commit an offence.[70]

Knowledge of the circumstances of the act incited

3.46 In Curr[71] the Court of Appeal held that D could only be guilty of inciting P if, were P to commit the act incited, P would do so with the requisite fault element to be convicted of the principal offence:

Example 3K

D, aged 40, encourages P, aged 18, to have sexual activity with V who is aged 15 but looks older.[72] D, besides knowing that V is aged 15, believes that P also thinks that V is 15. In fact, P, because of V's appearance and what she has told him, believes that V is aged 17. Just as P and D are about to embark on the sexual activity, V's mother interrupts them. She reports the matter to the police.

If Curr is applied to the facts of example 3K D would not be liable if P reasonably believed that V was 16 because P would not satisfy the fault element of the principal offence. Yet, D knows that V is aged 15 and, in addition, D believes that P believes that V is 15. Curr is an unsatisfactory decision because it focuses on P's rather than D's state of mind. In principle, D ought to be liable provided that:

(1) he or she *believes* that if P commits the act incited P would do so with the fault required for conviction of the offence; or

---

[67] *Criminal Law* (11th ed 2005) pp 353 to 354.

[68] *Marlow* [1997] *Criminal Law Review* 897.

[69] *Higgins* (1801) 2 East 5, 102 ER 269.

[70] On one view, *Invicta Plastics Ltd v Clare* [1976] RTR 251 also supports this proposition.

[71] [1968] 2 QB 944.

[72] It is an offence under s 9 of the Sexual Offences Act 2003 for P to have sexual activity with a child under 16 if P does not reasonably believe that the child is 16 or over.

(2)   D's own state of mind is such that, were he or she to commit the act incited, he or she would do so with that fault.

Whether P in fact satisfies the fault requirement should be irrelevant.

3.47   Equally unsatisfactory is the decision of the Court of Appeal in *Shaw*.[73] D encouraged a fellow employee to accept bogus invoices and issue cheques upon them. D did so in order to expose his employer's lax accounting systems. The Court held that D was not guilty of inciting P to obtain property by deception because, although P was acting dishonestly and D knew that he was, D's motive was not dishonest.

3.48   In his commentary on *Shaw*, Professor Sir John Smith said "the court has confused the mens rea of incitement with the mens rea of the offence incited",[74] a criticism that is equally applicable to *Curr*. Recently the Court of Appeal has said that the approach of the Court in *Curr* was wrong and that the mens rea of the person incited is "irrelevant".[75] However, since the Court of Appeal acknowledged that its ruling on the issue was unnecessary for its decision, the law remains as stated in *Curr*.

Defences

Withdrawal

3.49   Incitement is committed as soon as P is aware of D's encouragement. Thereafter, it is too late for D to withdraw the encouragement because the offence is already complete.

Crime prevention

3.50   Whether acting in order to prevent the commission of an offence is a defence to secondary liability and inchoate offences, including incitement, is unclear. The draft Criminal Code Bill provides for a defence to secondary liability where D acts "with the purpose of preventing the commission of an offence"[76] or "with the purpose of avoiding or limiting any harmful consequences of the offence and without the purpose of furthering its commission".[77]

---

[73]   [1994] *Criminal Law Review* 365.

[74]   Above, 366.

[75]   *C* [2005] EWCA Crim 2817 [30]. Previously the Divisional Court in *DPP v Armstrong* [2000] *Criminal Law Review* 379 had sought to distinguish both *Curr* and *Shaw*. Professor Sir John Smith described the Court's attempt to distinguish them as "unconvincing" – [2000] *Criminal Law Review* 380.

[76]   Clause 27(6)(a).

[77]   Clause 27(6)(b).

3.51   In the context of secondary liability, the authors of the draft Criminal Code Bill could point to *Clarke*.[78] D joined other burglars once an offence of burglary had been planned. He claimed that that he did so in order to ensure that the property stolen in the course of the burglary would be recovered. The Court of Appeal held that this could form the basis of a defence if the jury was satisfied that D's conduct was "overall calculated and intended not to further but to frustrate the ultimate result of the crime".[79]

3.52   By contrast, there is no direct authority on whether acting to prevent crime is a defence to incitement. We have explained that in *Shaw*[80] the Court of Appeal held that D was not guilty of incitement by encouraging P to commit offences of obtaining property by deception because D had not acted dishonestly. D's motive was not to prevent the commission of crime but merely to expose inefficiency. It might be thought, therefore, that the Court would have concluded that the case for exculpating D would have been even stronger had he been acting in order to prevent crime.

3.53   *Shaw* should be contrasted with *Smith*.[81] D offered a bribe to an official in order to expose corrupt practices in the local council. D was charged with and convicted of corruptly offering an inducement to an official.[82] The Court of Appeal upheld the conviction. D had acted "corruptly" because it was his intention that the official should enter into a corrupt bargain. The fact that D was not acting dishonestly was irrelevant.

3.54   *Smith* can be distinguished from *Shaw* in that in *Smith* D was charged with a substantive and not an inchoate offence. However, the Privy Council has held that it is no defence to a charge of conspiracy that an undercover drug enforcement officer who entered into a conspiracy to export heroin did so in order to expose the operation.[83] We agree with Professor Ashworth's description of the current law - "in confusion".[84]

---

[78] (1984) 80 Cr App R 344.

[79] Above, 347 to 348.

[80] [1994] *Criminal Law Review* 365.

[81] [1960] 2 QB 423.

[82] Contrary to the Public Bodies Corrupt Practices Act 1889, s 1.

[83] *Yip Chiu-Cheung v R* [1995] 1 AC 111. The Privy Council so ruled in upholding the defendant's conviction. The defendant had argued that he could not be guilty of conspiracy if the officer was not guilty of the offence. The officer was never prosecuted for the offence.

[84] *Principles of Criminal Law* (4th ed 2003) p 441.

Impossibility

3.55 The defence of impossibility is peculiar to inchoate offences. At common law, impossibility was capable of being a defence to attempt, conspiracy and incitement. However, by virtue of the Criminal Law Act 1977[85] and the Criminal Attempts Act 1981,[86] impossibility is no longer a defence to statutory conspiracies and attempts respectively.[87]

3.56 By contrast, it is the common law that continues to govern the defence of impossibility for common law conspiracies[88] and incitement.[89] The general principle is that impossibility is a defence to incitement unless the impossibility is merely the result of the inadequacy of the means to be used to commit the principal offence:

Example 3L

D encourages P to murder V. However, unknown to D, V is already dead.

Since V is dead, D is inciting P to do something that it is impossible to do. D is not guilty of incitement to murder.[90]

3.57 By contrast:

Example 3M

D gives P a jemmy and urges P to break into V's safe and steal a diamond. The diamond is in the safe but it would be impossible to break into the safe using the jemmy that D has provided.[91]

D cannot plead impossibility because the only reason why the offence cannot be committed is because the jemmy is an insufficient tool for breaking into the safe. This is right because the effectiveness of any assistance that D provides should be irrelevant in determining liability for an offence that is founded upon encouragement rather than assistance.

3.58 The defence of impossibility is not available in cases where D incites P to commit an offence that it is possible for P to commit, albeit only at some time in the future:

---

[85] Section 1(1)(b).

[86] Section 1(2) and (3).

[87] The leading case on the proper interpretation of the Criminal Attempts Act, s 1(2) and (3) is *Shivpuri [*1987] AC 1 overruling *Anderton v Ryan* [1985] AC 560.

[88] *DPP v Nock* [1978] AC 979.

[89] In *Fitzmaurice* [1983] QB 1083 the Court of Appeal said that the principles to be applied were those laid down by the House of Lords in *Haughton v Smith* [[1975] AC 476, a case decided when attempt was a common law offence.

[90] However, if D was aware that V was dead, D could be convicted of inciting attempted murder. A person can commit an offence by attempting to do the impossible – Criminal Attempts Act 1981, s 1(2). Inciting P to attempt the impossible is not the same as inciting P to do the impossible – see example 3H above at para 3.38.

[91] The example is taken from Smith and Hogan, *Criminal Law* (11th ed 2005) p 421.

Example 3N

D encourages P to murder, when it is born, her as yet unborn child.

D is guilty of incitement to murder.[92]

---

[92] *Shepherd* [1919] 2 KB 125. See also *McDonough* (1962) 47 Cr App R 37.

PART 4
THE CASE FOR AND AGAINST INCHOATE LIABILITY FOR ASSISTING THE COMMISSION OF AN OFFENCE

INTRODUCTION

4.1 In Part 3 we suggested that a major defect of the common law is the lack of inchoate liability for assisting the commission of an offence. In this Part we set out the competing arguments and explain why we are persuaded that the law of England and Wales would be improved were there to be such liability.

4.2 We acknowledge that the lack of a general inchoate liability for assisting the commission of an offence is not peculiar to the common law of England and Wales. Thus, neither the Canadian Criminal Code nor the New Zealand Crimes Act 1961 provides for such liability.

4.3 On the other hand, some jurisdictions do recognise inchoate liability for assisting crime. Macaulay's Indian Penal Code of 1860 contained an inchoate offence of abetment that covered both acts of encouragement and acts of assistance.[1] The American Law Institute's Modern Penal Code goes down a different route. A person who engages in conduct, designed to aid another to commit an offence, which would render him or her an accessory if the offence were committed, is guilty of an attempt to commit the offence even though the offence is not committed or attempted.[2] Further, if P does commit or attempt the offence but without reference to D's assistance,[3] D is an accessory to P's offence.[4]

THE ARGUMENTS IN FAVOUR OF INCHOATE LIABILITY FOR ASSISTING

Combating serious crime

4.4 The police would be able to work more effectively, particularly in the context of serious organised crime. Under the common law, the police cannot proceed against D until another person has committed or attempted to commit the principal offence. The lack of a general inchoate liability for assisting crime sits uneasily with the developments in intelligence-led policing which is now an important weapon in the state's response to serious organised crime. A general inchoate offence that capturing all preliminary acts of assistance regardless of whether the principal offence was subsequently committed or attempted would be a valuable addition to the state's resources in tackling serious organised crime.

---

[1] Section 107. This section is still in force in some jurisdictions.

[2] Article 5.01(3). According to the Comment at 314 (1985) "attempted complicity ought to be criminal, and to distinguish it from effective complicity appears unnecessary where the crime has been committed".

[3] As in example 3B in Part 3 above.

[4] Article 2.06 (3)(a)(ii).

The rationale underlying inchoate liability

4.5   Incitement, conspiracy and attempt, although distinct offences, share a common rationale. Each offence, by proscribing conduct that manifests an intention to bring about harm and enhances the prospect of harm occurring, enables the criminal law to intervene at a stage before the harm materialises. The utilitarian rationale underlying these offences is that the benefits of avoiding harm outweigh any disadvantages arising from what some might perceive as the criminal law's premature intervention. We believe that the utilitarian rationale is as strong when D's conduct consists of assisting as it is when D is encouraging or conspiring with P to bring about harm.

Eliminating the element of chance

4.6   In the CP, the Commission stated:

> Under the present law it is a matter of chance, so far as D is concerned, whether he becomes guilty, that chance depending on whether P commits the principal crime.[5]

It might be thought that criminal liability for culpable conduct that assists others to commit offences should not be a matter of chance or luck.

Sufficiently culpable conduct

4.7   Assisting another person to commit an offence is sufficiently culpable conduct to warrant the imposition of criminal liability even if that person does not commit or attempt to commit the offence. If D lends a gun to P so that P can and does murder V, we do not hesitate to label D's conduct as culpable. It is no less culpable merely because P for whatever reason does not commit the murder. As Professor Spencer has observed:

> It is no fault of mine – or to be more accurate, it is not due to any lack of fault on my part – that the crime was never committed. If my behaviour was bad enough to punish where you actually made use of the help I gave you, it was surely bad enough to punish where I fully expected you to use it but you got caught before you had the chance.[6]

Deterrence

4.8   An inchoate offence of facilitation may have some deterrent effect. It would deter some individuals from assisting prospective perpetrators of offences if they were aware that there was an immediate risk of liability regardless of whether the offence they were assisting was committed or attempted.

---

[5]   Para 4.39.

[6]   "Trying to help another person commit an offence" in P. Smith (ed) *Criminal Law, Essays in Honour of J C Smith* (1987) 148.

A more coherent approach

4.9 The lack of a general inchoate offence of assisting crime has resulted in a piecemeal and haphazard approach. Having noted that there are numerous statutory offences that criminalise particular acts of assisting, Professor Spencer stated:

> The present range of offences is quite inadequate to cover all the cases which ought to be covered, and the gaps between them produce some anomalies which suggest the criminal law has a very odd set of values. It is an offence under s 59 of the Offences Against the Person Act 1861 to lend a knitting needle for an abortion, for example, but no offence at all to lend a knife to commit murder – unless of course the murder is attempted or committed.[7]

Labelling and punishment

4.10 In addition, the current piecemeal approach, besides being neither comprehensive nor rational, may inadequately label or punish D for his or her conduct. Thus, even where a statutory provision does criminalise a preliminary act of assistance, it may fail to adequately label and punish D for what he or she has sought to encourage or assist:

Example 4A

D goes to P's home and sells P a swordstick believing that P intends to use it to murder P's wife. Before P can attempt to kill his wife, he is arrested.

D is guilty only of the statutory offence of selling an offensive weapon.[8] It is a summary offence, punishable with a maximum term of six months' imprisonment.

Restoring the proper boundaries of offences

4.11 The introduction of general inchoate liability for assisting crime would facilitate the process of restoring the proper boundaries of other inchoate offences, for example statutory conspiracy.

THE ARGUMENTS AGAINST INCHOATE LIABILITY FOR ASSISTING

Liability for otherwise lawful conduct

4.12 Marginal activities, that would otherwise constitute lawful conduct, would qualify as criminal assistance. Professor K J M Smith posits this example:

> D, a publican, or a generous host, believes that P is going to leave the premises in his car, but continues to ply him with drink to an extent that puts him well over the statutory limit. P does not in the event drive home.[9]

---

[7] Above, 158.

[8] Contrary to the Criminal Justice Act 1988, s 141.

[9] "The Law Commission Consultation Paper on Complicity: (1) A Blueprint for Rationalism" [1994] *Criminal Law Review* 239, 241.

Premature intervention

4.13 It would result in premature intervention and might result in D being liable for assisting P who had no intention of committing an offence. In his response to the CP, Professor Sir John Smith provided an example of D supplying a weapon to P in the belief that P will use it to murder V whereas P merely intends to shoot rabbits. In the CP, the Commission cited the example of D agreeing to pay P, a builder doing repairs to his house, in cash knowing or believing that P wants payment in this form to assist him in defrauding the Inland Revenue. P subsequently makes a proper return to the revenue as he had always intended to.[10]

Disparity between the liability of P and D

4.14 D will incur immediate liability for assisting P even though P, who may have requested the assistance, incurs no liability until he or she makes an attempt to commit the principal offence. In other words, there is a disparity between D and P. Professor Sir John Smith, in his response to the CP, expressed this concern:

> ... a gunsmith sells a shotgun to P, believing that P wants the gun to commit murder. D thereby commits the proposed offence of assisting murder and becomes liable to life imprisonment. ... . Even if P did intend to commit murder, however, he commits no offence by buying the gun. It is a " merely preparatory" act for which no criminal liability is imposed. There has been no agreement with D to commit murder so D and P have not committed the crime of conspiracy. So P who intended to commit murder and bought a gun for that purpose is not guilty of anything but D who believed he was assisting in the commission of murder by P is guilty of a very serious offence. ... . Buying a gun with an actual intent to use it to commit murder seems rather worse and more dangerous than selling a gun to one who is believed to intend to commit that offence. ... . While acts preparatory to the commission of an offence remain outside the criminal law, it is difficult to see how assisting such acts can fairly be brought within it.

Vagueness and uncertainty

4.15 On one view, an inchoate offence of assisting with no requirement of knowledge or belief as to the future commission of any specific offence, but related to crime in general, would make the requirements for liability unduly vague and uncertain. On the other hand, a test of knowledge or belief in respect of a particular offence would give rise to problems in cases where assistance is provided and no principal offence is subsequently committed. It might be very difficult to prove that P had a particular offence in mind. The Crown Prosecution Service ("the CPS"), in its response to the CP, provided an example. D supplies P with a baseball bat in the belief that P will use it commit an offence. The CPS pointed out that P could use the bat to commit one or more of eleven potential offences and that those offences do not proscribe the same conduct or result and do not have an identical fault element.

---

[10] Para 4.32.

4.16   The CPS believed that any requirement that D's fault must relate to a particular offence would be "highly unrealistic" because frequently D's state of mind would be "diffuse". Sir Edwin Jowitt, in his response to the CP, was of the same view:

> The armourer who hires out a weapon may not be told by the criminal what crime is afoot. The armourer may prefer not to know. He may be indifferent as to whether this, that or any crime is committed providing he receives his hire. The criminal may take the view that the less the armourer knows the better.

ADDRESSING THE OBJECTIONS

Liability for otherwise lawful conduct

4.17   Under the current law, a publican or generous host, D, who supplies alcohol to P may incur secondary liability if P commits or attempts to commit the offence of driving with excess alcohol. This is so even if D is indifferent as to whether P commits or attempts to commit the offence. It suffices that D believes that P will be driving with an amount of alcohol over the prescribed limit as a result of the alcohol dispensed by D.[11]

4.18   We acknowledge that to hold D criminally liable where P does not commit or attempt to commit the principal offence would constitute an extension of existing liability. We believe, however, that the mere fact that P does not commit or attempt to commit the principal offence does not in itself indicate that D's conduct is less deserving of punishment than if P had committed or attempted to commit the offence:

Example 4B

D1 and D2 hold a party. Among the guests are P1 and P2. Each drives to the party and both D1 and D2 believe, correctly, that P1 and P2 intend to drive home. D1 replenishes P1's glass with modest amounts of alcohol. D1 is aware that the alcohol he has dispensed, although modest, is such that P1 is over the statutory limit. D2 does likewise in respect of P2, the only difference being that the amount of alcohol she dispenses is far greater. P1 drives home and is stopped by the police. P1 is over the statutory limit and is charged with driving with excess alcohol.[12] P2 is so drunk that he collapses as he is about to leave to go home. Another guest at the party puts up P2 for the night and informs the police of the behaviour of D2.

By chance, P2 has not committed any offence whereas P1 has. At present, D1 is guilty of P1's offence as an accessory but D2 is not guilty of any offence. Yet, D2's conduct is as culpable as D1's, if not more so.

---

[11]   There is some authority to suggest that D is secondarily liable even if he merely foresaw that P might commit the principal offence – *Blakely and Sutton v DPP* [1991] RTR 405; *Reardon* [1999] *Criminal Law Review* 392. More recently, the Court of Appeal has suggested that the test is whether D foresaw that it was likely that P would commit the principal offence – *Webster* [2006] EWCA Crim 415.

[12]   Contrary to the Road Traffic Act 1988, s 5(1)(a).

4.19 Under our proposals for reform of secondary liability, a publican or host would be an accessory to P's offence of driving with excess alcohol only if it was his or her intention that P should commit the offence or be encouraged to commit the offence.[13] Most publicans and hosts do not supply alcohol to their customers or guests with the intention that the latter should drive with excess alcohol or that they should be encouraged to do so. However, they will often be aware that, as a result of supplying the alcohol, the customers and guests *will* be driving when in excess of the prescribed limit. In such cases, we see no reason why publicans and hosts should not be inchoately liable for assisting P to commit the offence.

Premature intervention

4.20 We are not persuaded by this objection. It is an objection that can be levelled at all the existing preliminary offences, including incitement. We are not aware, however, that it has been suggested that the law intervenes prematurely in cases where, for example, D encourages P to murder V but P has no intention of murdering V because, unknown to D, V is a relative of P.

4.21 The objection underestimates the importance of deterring and otherwise preventing crime. It implies that a person who is prepared to assist others to commit offences should be free to continue to do so with impunity until one of those persons commits or attempts to commit an offence. The objection would prevent persons being prosecuted when their intentions have been discovered by officials acting under-cover who wish to intervene before any principal offence is committed or attempted. We do not believe that it would be unduly intrusive or a waste of resources for the criminal law to intervene even in cases where P never intended to commit the offence that D was seeking to assist. Indeed, it would be a waste of resources should the law not be able to intervene.

Disparity between the liability of D and P

4.22 We acknowledge that it might be thought to be unfair for D and not P to be liable in circumstances where, at the time the assistance is rendered, P intends to commit the principal offence but for one or other reason does not commit or attempt to commit it.[14]

---

[13] An example would be if D and P had both applied for a job requiring the holder to hold a current driving licence. D invites P to dinner and, knowing that P will be driving home, provides P with copious amounts of alcohol. As D hoped, P is breathalysed and subsequently convicted of driving with excess alcohol. D is disqualified from holding or obtaining a driving licence.

[14] If D assists P in the mistaken belief that P will commit an offence there is no force in the objection. If P never intended to commit the offence, P cannot and should not incur liability.

4.23   Professor Sir John Smith's response to the CP[15] is a reminder of a fundamental principle of the common law of England and Wales, namely that it is not an offence to harbour an intention to commit an offence. The position may alter, however, if a person does something to manifest his or her intention to commit an offence.[16] However, at common law there is no *general* principle that doing an act that manifests an intention to bring about harm, but which is no more than merely preparatory to the commission of an offence, gives rise to criminal liability.[17]

4.24   Aside from the inchoate offences of attempt, conspiracy and incitement, the approach of English law has been to criminalise particular manifestations of an intention to commit an offence. Examples are possession of a firearm with intent to endanger life or injure property[18] and possession of an article intending to use it to destroy or damage property.[19] In this respect there is a similarity with the way in which the law has criminalised acts that assist others to commit offences. The approach has been piecemeal.

4.25   Our conclusion is that, although Professor Sir John Smith was right to highlight the fact that inchoate liability for assisting has the potential to render D criminally liable in situations where P either incurs no criminal liability or liability for a lesser offence, this is not a compelling objection. First, the objection cuts both ways. Arguably, what is needed is a form of *general* criminal liability for doing an act with the intention of bringing about harm.[20] Secondly, there is a difference between the actions of D and P. If D sells P a weapon that D correctly believes P will use to murder V, D has done everything that that he or she intends to do. Nothing more turns on D's subsequent conduct whereas P has yet to take the step of attempting to commit the offence. Professor Spencer has described P as:

> ... still a long way from his objective, and [having] a number of psychological barriers to cross before he reaches it, at any one of which he may change his mind and abandon his wicked plan.[21]

---

[15] See para 4.14.

[16] In his response, Professor Sir John Smith implied that all acts preparatory to the commission of an offence are outside the scope of the criminal law. However, this is not so. In the example that he provided, P having bought and taken possession of the gun would have committed an offence contrary to the Firearms Act 1968, s 16.

[17] If a person does an act that is more than merely preparatory to the commission of an offence, he or she may be guilty of attempt – Criminal Attempts Act 1981, s 1.

[18] Contrary to the Firearms Act 1968, s 16.

[19] Contrary to the Criminal Damage Act 1971, s 3.

[20] Whether there should be a general inchoate offence of doing anything, or being in possession of anything, with the intention of bringing about harm is beyond the remit of this project.

[21] "Trying to help another person commit a crime" in Smith, ed, *Criminal Law, Essays in Honour of JC Smith (1987)* 148 at p 159.

4.26 Thirdly, under our recommendations, if P approaches D for assistance in committing an offence, P *will* incur criminal liability. We are recommending that it should be an offence to do an act, with the requisite fault element, capable of encouraging or assisting another person to commit an offence. Accordingly if P asks D to supply him or her with an article so that P can commit an offence, P is doing an act capable of encouraging D to do an act capable of assisting P to commit an offence. In other words, if D supplies the article to P, not only is D committing the clause 2 offence but, by encouraging D to commit the clause 2 offence, P is committing the clause 1 offence.

Vagueness and uncertainty

4.27 This is an objection that we will address in Part 5[22] when discussing the fault elements of the offences that we are recommending.

CONCLUSIONS

4.28 We do not believe that the objections to a general inchoate liability for assisting crime withstand scrutiny. However, they do raise important issues as to what should be the appropriate fault element for the offences that we are recommending.[23]

4.29 Importantly, we believe that criminalising conduct that assists others to commit offences, irrespective of whether or not those offences are subsequently committed or attempted, will enhance and reinforce the ability of law enforcement agencies to tackle serious organised crime.

---

[22] Paras 5.90 to 5.99 below.

[23] We consider this in Part 5 paras 5.71 to 5.126 below.

PART 5
A SCHEME OF INCHOATE LIABILITY FOR ENCOURAGING OR ASSISTING THE COMMISSION OF OFFENCES

INTRODUCTION

5.1 In this Part and in Part 6[1] we set out the scheme of inchoate liability that we are recommending. At its core are two offences distinguished by different fault elements. We begin by briefly outlining the structure of the scheme that the Commission proposed in the CP. Then, we set out the general features of the scheme that we are now recommending. Finally, we consider how the offences that we are recommending should be defined.

THE STRUCTURE OF THE SCHEME PROPOSED IN THE CP

5.2 In the CP, the Commission provisionally proposed that there should be two inchoate offences to replace the common law inchoate offence of incitement and secondary liability.[2] The two offences were:

    (1)   encouraging crime,[3] and

    (2)   assisting crime.[4]

5.3 There were two reasons why the Commission distinguished the two offences in the way that it did. First, the Commission believed that "encouraging" and "assisting" were two separate activities.[5] Secondly, it believed that the fault element for encouraging crime should be narrower than that for assisting crime:

> If D's conduct can truly be said to assist the commission of crime, and he is aware that that is so, then there are strong arguments for imposing legal inhibitions upon it, even though the giving of such assistance was not D's purpose. Where, however, D's conduct is not of assistance to P, but merely emboldens or fortifies P in committing a crime, it seems to extend the law too far to make D's conduct itself criminal, unless D intended it to have that effect.[6]

---

[1]   In Part 6 we consider defences and exemptions.

[2]   Subject to possibly retaining some form of accessorial liability for collateral offences committed by P in the course of a joint venture.

[3]   Para 4.163.

[4]   Para 4.99.

[5]   Para 4.10.

[6]   Para 4.154.

THE GENERAL FEATURES OF THE INCHOATE SCHEME THAT WE ARE RECOMMENDING

The new offences

5.4 The scheme that we are recommending also comprises two core offences ("the new offences"). They are set out in clauses 1(1) and 2(1) of the draft Crime (Encouraging and Assisting) Bill ("the Bill") that is appended to this report. The offences are:

(1) **encouraging or assisting the commission of a criminal act *intending* that the criminal act should be committed ("the clause 1 offence"), and**

(2) **encouraging or assisting the commission of a criminal act *believing* that the encouragement or assistance will encourage or assist the commission of the criminal act and believing that the criminal act will be committed ("the clause 2(1) offence").** [7]

5.5 We envisage that the new offences would usually be charged in relation to a substantive offence, for example encouraging or assisting murder or encouraging or assisting rape. However, the clause 1 offence, but not the clause 2(1) offence, could also be charged in relation to:

(1) the clause 1 or the clause 2(1) offence, for example D encourages or assists P to encourage or assist X to murder V; and

(2) the inchoate offences of conspiracy and attempt, for example D encourages or assists P1 and P2 to form a conspiracy to murder V.[8]

5.6 The following examples illustrate the essential difference between the clause 1 offence and the clause 2(1) offence:

Example 5A

D believes that P is about to attack V who is D's worst enemy. D throws a brick to within P's reach in order to assist P in what D believes will be the attack on V. P makes no attempt to attack V.

Example 5B

P goes into D's hardware shop and chooses a large knife from the display. P tells D that he is going to use it to attack V. D knows P well and believes what P says. D nonetheless sells the knife to P, rationalising his action by telling himself that P is just another customer. In the event, P does not try to attack V.

---

[7] In addition, cl 2(2) of the Bill sets out an additional offence which can be explained more easily when the cl 2(1) offence has been explained.

[8] See Part 7 below.

In example 5A, D commits the clause 1 offence because D intended that P should assault V.[9] By contrast, in example 5B, D commits the clause 2(1) offence because D, without intending that P should assault V, believes that P will do so.[10]

5.7 The new offences would replace the common law offence of incitement[11] and would fill the existing gap at common law by introducing a general inchoate liability for assisting the commission of an offence provided the requisite fault element is satisfied.[12]

Potential overlap with secondary liability

5.8 The new offences can be committed whether or not the principal offence is committed.[13] In Part 2,[14] we said that we were persuaded that secondary liability should be retained to cater for cases where D encourages or assists P to commit an offence intending that P should commit the offence. Accordingly, there is a potential overlap between secondary liability and the clause 1 offence:

Example 5C

D encourages P to set fire to the local tax office.

If P decides not to set fire to the tax office, D can only be guilty of the clause 1 offence. D would not be an accessory to arson because P had not even attempted to commit the offence. On the other hand, were P to set fire to the premises, D, as well as committing the clause 1 offence, would be an accessory to arson[15] because it was D's intention that P should commit arson. The prosecution could choose to charge D with the clause 1 offence but we would expect that they would wish to charge D with arson.

---

[9] A connected but separate issue concerns the principal offence that D is guilty of intentionally encouraging or assisting – is it assault, assault occasioning actual bodily harm, maliciously inflicting grievous bodily harm or causing grievous bodily harm with intent? We consider this in paras 5.106 to 5.121 below.

[10] Again, the issue referred to in n 9 above will arise.

[11] Clause 13 of the Bill abolishes the common law offence of incitement. However, statutory offences of incitement are unaffected by the Bill.

[12] The fault elements for each of the new offences are contained in cl 1(2) and (3) and cl 2(3) and (4) respectively.

[13] Clause 3(1) of the Bill.

[14] Paras 2.22 to 2.23.

[15] Contrary to the Criminal Damage Act 1971, s 1(1) and (3).

5.9 By contrast, under our forthcoming proposals for reform of secondary liability, there is limited scope for overlap between secondary liability and the clause 2(1) offence because, subject to one exception,[16] D will not be secondarily liable in cases where it was not his or her intention that P should commit the principal offence or be encouraged or assisted to commit it:

Example 5D

D, a shopkeeper, sells petrol to P believing that P will use it to make a petrol bomb with which to commit arson. D is indifferent as to what P does with the petrol. P, as D anticipated, makes a petrol bomb and uses it to set fire to the tax office.

D is guilty of the clause 2(1) offence but is not an accessory to and guilty of arson.

Unknown mode of participation

5.10 If the principal offence is committed, it may not be possible for the prosecution to prove whether an accused was the perpetrator of the offence or, instead, encouraged or assisted its commission. In order to ensure that D does not escape liability, we believe that there should be a similar rule to that which is integral to secondary liability.[17]

5.11 **We recommend that If the prosecution can prove that D must either have perpetrated the clause 1 or the clause 2(1) offence, on the one hand, or encouraged or assisted its commission, on the other, D can be convicted of the clause 1 or the clause 2(1) offence.[18]**

The implications of the new offences being inchoate offences

5.12 The new offences are inchoate in that D's liability is not dependent on P committing or attempting to commit the principal offence. Accordingly, D's liability can only be fixed by reference to the offence that D intended or believed that he or she was encouraging or assisting. Importantly, the same is also true if P (or another person) *does* commit an offence with D's encouragement or assistance. The following four sections illustrate the application of this principle.

---

[16] Under our proposals, P would incur secondary liability for collateral offences that he or she foresaw *might* be committed in the course of a joint venture. However, foresight of a possibility that P might commit a collateral offence will not render D liable for the clause 2(1) offence. This is because, in order to be guilty of the clause 2(1) offence, D must believe that P *will* commit the offence. Therefore, the overlap between the clause 2(1) offence and secondary liability will be confined to cases where, in the course of a joint venture, P commits a collateral offence which D believed P *would* commit.

[17] See Part 2 paras 2.8 to 2.9

[18] Clause 10(1) of the Bill and see Appendix A paras A.80 to A.85.

D's liability is for encouraging or assisting an abstract and not a particular principal offence

5.13 D may not know the details of the prospective principal offence. Thus, D may provide P with a baseball bat believing that P will use it to rob V1. Instead, P uses it to rob V2. Alternatively, D may provide the baseball bat believing that P will use it to commit robbery but have no belief as to the identity of the victim. It matters not that D lacks knowledge or belief as to the details of the prospective principal offence. D is guilty of encouraging or assisting P to commit robbery rather than encouraging or assisting P to rob V.

The offence committed is not the offence that D believed would be committed

5.14 P may commit a different offence to that which D believed would be committed:

Example 5E

In return for payment, D provides P with a hunting knife believing that P is going to use it to commit robbery. Instead, P uses it to commit murder.

D is guilty of encouraging or assisting robbery. Had P been arrested before being able even to attempt to murder V, D would have been guilty of encouraging or assisting robbery because robbery was the offence that D believed P would commit with D's assistance. The nature and extent of D's liability should be and is unaffected by the fact that P commits an offence which is different from the offence which D believed P would commit. Conversely, had D believed that P would use the knife to commit murder, D would be guilty of encouraging or assisting murder even if, instead, P used the knife to commit robbery.

D's act of encouragement or assistance leads to the commission of multiple offences

5.15 In the context of secondary liability, a single act of encouragement or assistance leading to the commission of multiple offences gives rise, at least in theory, to a difficulty:

Example 5F

In return for payment, D provides P with a jemmy believing that P will use it to commit a burglary at V's premises. P uses the jemmy to burgle not only V's premises but also the premises of X, Y and Z.

Arguably, under the current law D is an accessory to and guilty of all four burglaries. In *Bainbridge*[19] the Court of Criminal Appeal held that, in order to convict D of an offence as an accessory, it was sufficient to prove that the offence committed by P was of the same type as that which D believed P would commit. In example 5F, all four offences committed by P are the type of offence that D believed P would commit.

---

[19] [1960] 1 QB 129.

5.16 The issue does not arise in the context of the new offences that we are recommending. Again, this reflects the nature of inchoate liability. In example 5F, D would be liable for encouraging or assisting burglary even if P did not commit any of the burglaries. Conversely, the fact that P used the jemmy to commit four burglaries should not alter the nature and extent of D's liability. D is guilty of one offence of encouraging or assisting burglary because D believed that only one offence would be committed.

5.17 In example 5F, D believed that P would use the jemmy to commit one burglary. Instead, if D believed that P would use the jemmy to commit all four burglaries, D could be charged with four offences of encouraging or assisting burglary irrespective of how many of them P committed.[20] Our scheme ensures that D's liability reflects the nature and extent of the criminality that D either intended or expected to materialise from his or her encouragement or assistance. Accordingly, it would be open to a court to impose a more severe sentence on D1 who believed that P1 would commit 20 burglaries even if P1 commits none of them than on D2 who believes that P will commit a single burglary even if P2 does commit the offence.

A person other than P commits the offence that D has encouraged or assisted

5.18 Under our scheme, there is no requirement that if the offence that D has encouraged or assisted is committed, it must be committed by P:

> **Example 5G**
>
> D, in return for payment, provides P with cutting equipment believing that P will use it to commit a burglary. P is involved in a serious motor accident and, consequently, P's brother, X, uses the equipment to commit the burglary.

D is guilty of encouraging or assisting burglary. D would be guilty of the offence if no burglary was committed and it follows that if the offence is committed, it should be irrelevant who commits it.

DEFINING THE NEW OFFENCES

Introduction

5.19 Inchoate liability has the potential to condemn D even though no harm actually occurs and there was never any prospect that it would occur. Where the focus of potential criminal liability is conduct that might have led to harm but which cannot be shown to have caused or contributed to any actual harm, the state of mind required to ground liability assumes particular significance. Professor Ashworth has observed:

---

[20] Clause 3(2) of the Bill.

There is, however, some evidence of a general proposition that the inchoate offences should be subject to more restrictive principles than other crimes; thus intention and knowledge are generally required for the inchoate offence and recklessness is insufficient.[21]

With these cautionary words in mind, we consider what should be the conduct and fault elements of each of the new offences.

The conduct element

Introduction

5.20 Unlike the offences that the Commission proposed in the CP, the new offences that we are recommending share a common conduct element. There are two reasons. First, we no longer believe that encouraging and assisting are necessarily separate activities. We think that the concepts can overlap and that whether conduct is to be described as encouraging or assisting can sometimes involve drawing fine distinctions. P may be as likely to commit an offence because of the encouragement he or she derives from having the backing of D than as a result of the assistance that evidences that backing. There will be cases where the prosecution may want to put its case on the basis that D has done an act that was capable of either encouraging or of assisting, or both. We believe that it will be easier for the prosecution to do so if each offence can be committed by doing an act capable of "encouraging or assisting".

5.21 Secondly, even if encouraging and assisting were separate activities, we no longer believe that the fault element for encouraging crime should be narrower than the fault element for assisting crime.[22]

5.22 **We are recommending that the conduct element of both the clause 1 offence and the clause 2(1) offence should consist of *"do[ing] an act capable of encouraging or assisting the doing of a criminal act"*.[23]** In the sections that follow, we consider the different components of this conduct element.

---

[21] *Principles of Criminal Law*, (4th ed 2003) p 472.

[22] See paras 5.79 to 5.80 below.

[23] Clauses 1(1)(a) and 2(1)(a) of the Bill.

Criminal act

5.23   A criminal offence can consist of one or more of three external elements: conduct, the circumstances in which the conduct takes place and the consequences of the conduct.[24] However, although an offence can comprise all three elements, not all three elements are integral to the definition of every completed offence. Whether one, two or all three elements are part of the definition of an offence varies a great deal. Criminal damage is an offence[25] that has all three elements: conduct (for example throwing a stone), consequence (damaging or destroying property) and circumstance (property belonging to another).

5.24   Under the scheme that we recommend, "criminal act" refers to an act that falls within the definition of the conduct element of the principal offence.[26] It does not include the consequence element of the principal offence. Thus, in relation to murder "criminal act" is, for example, P's physical act in stabbing V. If D encourages P to stab V, D has done an act capable of encouraging D to do a criminal act.[27]

5.25   In most cases, the requirement that D's conduct must be capable of encouraging or assisting the conduct element of the principal offence will not cause any problems. However, occasionally, D's conduct will not be capable of encouraging or assisting the conduct element:

> **Example 5H**
>
> D and P have applied for a job that requires the holder to possess a valid driving licence. They attend a party. D surreptitiously "laces" P's non-alcoholic drinks with alcohol knowing that P intends to drive home. D's intention is that P should commit the offence of driving with excess alcohol and be disqualified from holding or obtaining a driving licence.[28] An off-duty policeman at the party notices what D is doing and advises P not to drive. P goes home in a taxi.

The conduct element of the offence of driving in excess of the prescribed limit is driving a motor vehicle. D's act of "lacing" D's drinks is not an act capable of encouraging or assisting P to drive. It is an act, however, that is capable of bringing about the circumstance element of the offence, namely, being in excess of the prescribed limit.

---

[24]   R A Duff, *Criminal Attempts* (1996) p 13 believes that this way of distinguishing the different elements of the actus reus is problematic because it is relative to the way that we describe actions. Thus, if a rapist's action is described as "having sexual intercourse" the victim's non-consent is a circumstance of the rapist's action. If the rapist's action is described as "having non-consensual sexual intercourse" the victim's non-consent is part of the action itself rather than a circumstance.

[25]   Criminal Damage Act 1971.

[26]   Clause 17(2) of the Bill – "an act (or failure to act) that falls within the definition of the act (or failure to act) that must be proved in order for a person to be convicted of the offence".

[27]   If, as a matter of law, P can perpetrate the conduct element of the principal offence by refraining from doing a positive act, D does an act capable of encouraging or assisting "the doing" of a criminal act by encouraging or assisting P to refrain from doing the positive act, eg D urges P to murder P's child, V, by starving V - cl 17(2) of the Bill.

[28]   Contrary to the Road Traffic Act 1988, s 5(1).

5.26 The essence of the wrongdoing targeted by the offence of driving with excess alcohol is not the driving but driving *in excess of the prescribed limit*. In example 5H, it is that circumstance that D is intending to bring about. D's conduct is highly culpable and, in principle, he or she ought to be criminally liable. Accordingly, on what we anticipate will be rare occasions, "criminal act" will need to be interpreted to mean a composite act comprising a combination of conduct and circumstance elements.

"Capable of" encouraging or assisting

5.27 Inchoate liability criminalises culpable conduct not because it results in actual harm but because it enhances the prospect of actual harm occurring. It threatens to bring about harm. Consistent with the rationale of inchoate liability, D's conduct need not in fact encourage or assist the doing of a criminal act. It is for this reason that the Bill merely requires that D does an act "capable of" encouraging or assisting the doing of a criminal act.

5.28 The question of whether D's conduct was capable of encouraging or assisting the doing of a criminal act is one of fact for juries and magistrates to determine. We do not believe that it is either necessary or desirable to construct a sub-structure of detailed rules for determining the question. We envisage that in most cases the question will not arise and that, when it does, juries or magistrates will have little difficulty in deciding the question:

Example 5J

D, having heard that P intends to commit a burglary, sends P a package believing that it contains D's notes on how to break into buildings. In fact, the package contains his mother's cookery recipes. P has no intention of committing burglary and reports the matter to the police.

The recipe notes were clearly not capable of encouraging or assisting the criminal act of entering a building as a trespasser and, therefore, D cannot be convicted of either the clause 1 or the clause 2(1) offence.[29]

5.29 However, one area of potential difficulty is whether an act can "be capable" of encouraging or assisting the doing of a criminal act if nobody is aware of the act. A person can in fact be assisted without being aware of the act of assistance.[30] It should follow therefore that an act "is capable" of assisting even if nobody is aware of the act:

---

[29] However, D could be convicted of attempting to encourage or assist P to commit burglary. In sending the package, D has done an act which is "more than merely preparatory" to the commission of the clause 1 offence or clause 2(1) offence – Criminal Attempts Act 1981, s 1(1). Further, the fact that it was impossible for P to be encouraged or assisted by the recipe notes will not avail D. Impossibility is not a defence to the inchoate offence of attempt – Criminal Attempts Act 1981, s 1(2).

[30] *State v Tally* (1894) 102 Ala 25.

> **Example 5K**
>
> D and V live in an area plagued by burglaries. V goes on holiday. D hears a rumour that unidentified persons are planning to burgle V's premises. D, who hates V, leaves a ladder by the side of V's premises intending that it should assist a burglary of V's premises. W sees P placing the ladder and reports the matter to the police.

The criminal act of burglary is entering a property as a trespasser. At the moment of placing the ladder, D has done an act "capable of" assisting the doing of the criminal act.

5.30 By contrast, a person cannot in fact be encouraged unless he or she is aware of the encouragement. However, we do not believe that it follows that, because *actual* encouragement requires an awareness of the encouragement, an act cannot be "capable of" encouraging unless and until it comes to someone's attention:

> **Example 5L**
>
> D posts a letter to P urging P to commit a serious assault on V. The letter is destroyed in a fire at the post office. Subsequently, D writes a letter to X in which he tells X of the contents of the letter to P. X informs the police.

It would be a question of fact for the jury whether D had done an act capable of encouraging or assisting the commission of murder or, instead, had merely attempted to do an act capable of encouraging or assisting P to commit the offence.[31]

5.31 We recognise that in some cases there may be an uncertain boundary between, on the one hand, doing an act capable of encouraging or assisting and, on the other, doing an act that is more than merely preparatory to doing so, that is attempting to do so. However, taking into account that the maximum sentence for each would be the same, we think that this is preferable to constructing an edifice of detailed and complicated rules to distinguish a completed act from an attempt, particularly as the issue will arise infrequently.

Encouraging

ENCOURAGING RATHER THAN INCITING

5.32 In the commentary on the draft Criminal Code Bill,[32] the Commission said that it had been persuaded that incite was preferable to encourage because encourage might be read as requiring the prosecution to prove actual encouragement.[33]

---

[31] Similarly, if P received the letter but did not open it or, having opened and read it, did not appreciate that D was encouraging him to assault V.

[32] A Criminal Code for England and Wales vol 2, Commentary on Draft Criminal Code Bill (1976) Law Com No 177.

[33] Above, para 13.6.

5.33 However, if, as we believe, it ought to be possible to commit the new offences without proof of P being in fact encouraged (or assisted),[34] this can be achieved without having to resort to "inciting". If the new offences can be committed by doing an act "capable of" encouraging or assisting, this precludes any argument that there has to be actual encouragement.

5.34 We prefer encouraging to inciting because, as the Commission pointed out in the CP, incite "has somewhat instigatory connotations".[35] As we explain below,[36] we believe that the new offences should capture conduct that is capable of emboldening or fortifying a person who has already made up his or her mind to commit an offence.

5.35 We do not think that the choice of encouraging will lead to uncertainty. In Marlow[37] the Court of Appeal, in considering the meaning of "incites", stated that " 'encourages' represents as well as any modern word can the concept involved."[38]

THE MEANING OF ENCOURAGING

5.36 There are two issues. One is identifying what conduct ought to be capable of amounting to encouraging. The other is whether it is necessary or desirable to provide a statutory definition of encouraging.

5.37 We believe that encouraging should have the same broad meaning that inciting has acquired at common law.[39] In particular, we agree with the provisional view expressed in the CP that encouraging should encompass not only instigating and persuading but also conduct that simply emboldens a person who has already decided to commit an offence.[40] We do so because, as the Commission said in the CP, to embolden P in his or her intention to commit an offence may not only inhibit repentance but is undesirable conduct that conflicts with the citizen's duty to uphold the law.[41] We also agree that to make D's liability depend on whether he or she sought to instigate the commission of an offence would result in infinite room for argument.[42]

---

[34] On which, see paras 5.27 to 5.31 above.

[35] Para 4.160. The CP was published before the decision in Goldman [200] Criminal Law Review 822.

[36] See para 5.37 below.

[37] [1997] Criminal Law Review 897.

[38] Above.

[39] In Goldman [2001] Criminal Law Review 822 it was held that "incitement" covered a suggestion, proposal, persuasion or inducement. In Giannetto [1997] 1 Cr App R 1, a case of secondary liability, the trial judge directed the jury that D would be liable as an accessory to the murder of V if P had suggested murdering V and D had replied "Oh goody". The Court of Appeal did not criticise the direction and said that "mere encouragement … would suffice".

[40] Para 4.148.

[41] Para 4.150.

[42] Para 4.149.

5.38 If encouragement should include conduct that emboldens or fortifies a person who has already decided to commit an offence, we do not believe that it should matter that P initiated the dialogue that led to D's encouragement. In *Goldman*[43] it was held that D had attempted to incite P to distribute indecent photographs of children by responding to an advertisement placed by P which invited readers to purchase the photographs. The decision has been criticised.[44] It is said to extend the natural meaning of incitement and, thereby, to enable a purchaser of controlled drugs to be liable for inciting his or her supplier at a point well in advance of incurring any liability for possession or attempted possession of the drugs.

5.39 We sympathise with the criticism to the extent that *Goldman* may have extended the natural meaning of incitement. It is for this reason that we prefer encouraging to inciting because D can clearly encourage P even though P has already made up his or her mind to commit an offence.

5.40 However, we disagree with the other aspect of the criticism. The law should seek to deter not only the possession of controlled drugs (and child pornography) but also its supply. Without purchasers there would be no suppliers of controlled drugs or child pornography. The purchaser, by emboldening and fortifying the supplier, is contributing to the evils and misery caused by the supply and consumption of controlled drugs and child pornography. As a matter of policy, it is desirable and necessary that consumers of controlled drugs and child pornography can be punished not only for possessing such merchandise but also for encouraging others to supply it.

5.41 Further, there would be no disparity between the liability of the supplier, P, and the liability of the purchaser, D. By responding positively to the supplier's offer to supply drugs, D is liable for encouraging or assisting P to commit the offence of supplying controlled drugs.[45] In turn, P is liable for encouraging or assisting D to encourage or assist P to supply controlled drugs.[46]

5.42 It is clear that at common law incitement can consist of threats and pressure.[47] Although it might be thought to be linguistically inappropriate to describe threatening or coercing as "encouraging", such conduct ought to be and is caught by the offences that we are recommending.[48] As Simester and Sullivan point out[49] there is no reason why an employer who persuades an employee to commit an offence by threatening redundancy should be in a better position than an employer whose persuasive technique is to offer a pay rise.

---

[43] [2001] Crim LR 822.

[44] Simester and Sullivan, *Criminal Law Theory and Doctrine* (2nd ed 2003) p 265.

[45] Contrary to the Misuse of Drugs Act 1971, s 4(1)(b).

[46] In addition, P would be liable for offering to supply a controlled drug – Misuse of Drugs Act 1971, s 4(1)(b).

[47] *Race Relations Board v Applin* [1973] QB 815.

[48] See cl 15(1) of the Bill.

[49] *Criminal Law Theory and Doctrine* (2nd ed 2003) pp 265-266.

5.43 **We recommend that the doing of an act capable of encouraging or assisting the doing of a criminal act should include doing so by threatening or pressurising another person to do a criminal act.**

5.44 The draft Criminal Code did not expand on the meaning of "incite". Likewise, we believe that it is unnecessary to expand on the meaning of encourage. It is a word in common usage and, if anything, is more familiar to juries and magistrates than "incite".

5.45 We are strengthened in our view by the fact that the meaning of incite has rarely troubled the courts. It is true that in the CP the Commission suggested[50] that there was uncertainty as to whether there had to be an element of persuasion or pressure. If there was any uncertainty,[51] it is now clear that there is no such requirement.[52]

Assisting[53]

THE MEANING OF ASSISTING

5.46 Unlike "encouraging", in the CP the Commission had no common law inchoate offence to draw upon when considering the meaning of "assisting". It said that assisting in its normal sense "extends to any conduct on the part of D that, as a matter of fact, makes it easier for P to commit the principal offence".[54] Having concluded that assisting is a "sufficient and satisfactory concept",[55] it suggested that assistance should include the giving of advice as to how to commit an offence and advice as to how P might avoid detection or apprehension.[56] The Commission invited comment on whether acts of insubstantial assistance should be excluded from the scope of the offence.[57]

---

[50] Para 2.133.

[51] The Commission itself said that specific authority for the view that there had to be persuasion or pressure was "notably sparse" - para 2.132.

[52] *Marlow* [1997] *Criminal Law Review* 897; *Goldman* [2001] *Criminal Law Review*.

[53] Owing to the fact that at common law there is no inchoate offence of assisting crime, the authorities on what constitutes "assisting" are cases, usually of complicity, in which the issue has been whether D has "aided" P to commit an offence.

[54] Para 4.71.

[55] Para 4.48.

[56] Para 4.99(2).

[57] Para 5.2.6(2).

ADVICE AS ASSISTANCE

5.47 In *A-G v Able*[58] the High Court held that the giving of advice was conduct capable of "aiding and abetting" for the purposes of secondary liability. In the CP the Commission noted[59] that the law had been strongly criticised because it "gives too great an extension to criminal complicity. If the writer of the letter was guilty the first time his information was used, he would be guilty the nth time, which is absurd"."[60]

5.48 Despite the criticism of *A-G v Able*, in the CP the Commission proposed that providing advice should be conduct capable of amounting to assisting. It emphasised[61] that insofar as there was a problem, it is associated with secondary rather than inchoate liability.

5.49 No respondent to the CP disagreed with the proposal that providing advice should be conduct that is capable of assisting. We continue to believe that it should be so regarded.

ACTS OF INSUBSTANTIAL ASSISTANCE

5.50 In the CP, the Commission said that if it was D's purpose to facilitate the commission of an offence, D should be liable whether or not the assistance was substantial.[62] We invited comment on whether liability should be limited to substantial assistance if the fault elements of the inchoate offence of assisting crime were to be extended beyond purpose or intention.[63]

---

[58] [1984] QB 795. The case involved the distribution of a leaflet describing ways of committing suicide. It was a civil case in which the Attorney-General sought a declaration that publication of the booklet would constitute an offence because it would "aid and abet" suicide contrary to s 2(1) of the Suicide Act 1961.

[59] Para 4.53.

[60] Glanville Williams, *Criminal Law: The General Part* (2nd ed 1960) p 381 criticising the New Zealand case of *Baker* (1909) 28 NZLR 536 where D was held liable as a party to an offence because he had written a letter describing in general terms techniques for safe-breaking. It should be noted that the problem that Professor Williams adverted to is not confined to advice. A jemmy can be used to commit numerous burglaries.

[61] Para 4.154.

[62] Para 4.66.

[63] Para 4.67.

5.51   The majority of respondents thought that it should be irrelevant whether the assistance was substantial. We agree. Inchoate liability is not dependent on the commission of a substantive offence. D's liability turns not on what P does but on what D intends or believes will be the impact of his or her conduct. We think that to introduce such a requirement would lead to uncertainty and difficulty. It would require juries and magistrates to "seek to assess how extensive a contribution the assistance would have been (or was) in bringing about the principal offence".[64] Accordingly, D should be liable if his or her act is capable of assisting (or encouraging) another person to any extent. The marginal nature of any assistance or encouragement can be reflected in the sentence.[65]

Must D's encouragement or assistance be directed at a particular person or persons?

5.52   The issue is most likely to arise in relation to encouragement. There should be no requirement that D has any particular individual(s) or group(s) as the target of his or her encouragement. If D posts a message on a web-site urging the assassination of all immigrants, he or she ought to be liable regardless of whether the encouragement is aimed at a particular individual, a group of individuals or the world at large.

Omissions as acts capable of encouraging or assisting

5.53   Determining the circumstances in which a person should incur criminal liability for an omission involves difficult policy issues. In the context of secondary liability, Professor Ashworth says the key issue is simple to state: "can a person be convicted as an accomplice merely for standing by and doing nothing when an offence is being committed"?[66]

5.54   The general rule at common law is that a person incurs no criminal liability for standing by and doing nothing. The reluctance of the law to impose criminal liability for omissions is attributable to a number of reasons of which perhaps the most significant is that:

> The prohibition of omissions is far more intrusive upon the individuals' autonomy and freedom than is the prohibition of acts, which is why the systematic imposition of (criminal or civil) liability for failures to act is to be resisted.[67]

---

[64]   Professor K J M Smith, "The Law Commission Consultation Paper on Complicity (1): A Blueprint for Rationalism" [1994] *Criminal Law Review* 239, 243.

[65]   With one exception, we are recommending that D should be liable to any penalty for which for which he or she would be liable if convicted of the principal offence. The exception is if D is convicted or encouraging or assisting murder. D would be liable to a maximum sentence of imprisonment for life but would not attract the mandatory life sentence – cl 12(2) of the Bill.

[66]   *Principles of Criminal Law* (4th ed 2003) p 418.

[67]   Simester and Brookbanks, *Principles of Criminal Law* (2nd ed 2002) p 46.

5.55   However, the general rule of common law is subject to an important exception. Provided an offence is capable of being committed by inaction, a person may commit the offence if he or she is under a duty to act but refrains from doing so.[68] In the context of secondary liability, the law has focused on three issues:

(1)   the extent to which and the circumstances in which D can incur secondary liability by virtue of mere presence when P commits an offence;

(2)   whether D can incur secondary liability by failing to take steps to discharge a duty;[69] and

(3)   whether D can incur secondary liability by failing to exercise an entitlement to prevent or control the actions of P.[70]

5.56   The law in relation to (1) is reasonably clear:

> **Example 5M**
>
> D is on a bus when a passenger P starts to assault another passenger V. D remains in his seat and continues to read his newspaper.

D, provided that he takes no positive action to encourage or assist P, is not an accessory to the assault because he under no legal obligation to act in order to prevent P assaulting V.

> **Example 5N**
>
> D comes across P who is about to rape V. V pleads for D to help her but D passes by. P rapes V.

Again, D incurs no criminal liability for declining to go to V's aid. By contrast, if D takes the positive step of stopping in order to watch P rape V, a jury is entitled, but not bound, to find that D intended to encourage P and that D in fact encouraged P.[71]

5.57   The law in relation to (2) is also reasonably clear. If D is under a duty to act, then D can incur secondary liability for an offence committed by P as a result of D failing to take steps to discharge the duty, provided that P is thereby encouraged or assisted to commit the offence.

---

[68]   *Gibbins and Proctor* (1918) 13 Cr App R 134; *Pittwood* (1902) 19 TLR 37.

[69]   A parent is under a legal duty to act in order to ensure the health and safety of his or child. A police officer is under a similar duty towards those whom he or she has arrested or who are in his or her custody. A legal duty to act may arise because of a contractual relationship, eg employer and employee.

[70]   The owner of a motor car is entitled to control the actions of those whom he or she allows to drive the car – *Du Cros v Lambourne* [1907] 1 KB 40. An owner of premises or land is entitled to control the actions of those who are on the premises or land.

[71]   The relevant authorities are *Coney* (1882) 8 QBD 534; *Wilcox v Jeffery* [1951] 1 All ER 464; *Allen* [1965] 1 QB 130; *Smith v Baker* [1971] 1 RTR 350; *Clarkson* [1971] 1 WLR 1402; *Allen v Ireland* [1984] 1 WLR 903; *Bland* [1988] Criminal Law Review 41.

5.58 The law in relation to (3) is far less clear. There have been specific instances where the courts have held D to be secondarily liable for failing to control the actions of others.[72] However, it is open to question whether any general principle can be derived from those cases.[73]

THE PROPOSALS IN THE CP

5.59 In the CP, the Commission distinguished encouraging, on the one hand, and assisting, on the other. It provisionally concluded that it ought not to be possible to assist crime by failing to discharge a duty or by failing to exercise an entitlement right of authority to prevent or control the actions of P.[74] The justification for this limitation was threefold. First, it would bring certainty. Secondly, it would prevent the defence being unreasonably wide. Finally, it would mean that the offence would be in line with the general principles of the criminal law.

5.60 By contrast, the Commission provisionally concluded that the proposed inchoate offence of encouraging crime could be committed by inaction.[75] The Commission thought that it would not be unreasonable, or make the law dangerously wide, if encouraging encompassed omissions.

RESPONSES TO THE PROPOSALS IN THE CP

5.61 The majority of respondents who addressed this issue did not accept the proposition that failing to discharge a duty to prevent or control P's actions should never be regarded as "assisting".

CONCLUSIONS AND RECOMMENDATIONS

Failure to discharge a duty

5.62 In principle, we believe that the new offences should be capable of being committed by virtue of inaction on the part of D that consists of refraining from taking steps to discharge a duty. Confining liability to positive acts would result in D incurring no criminal liability in situations where he or she ought to, for example D, a disgruntled security guard, who fails to turn on a burglar alarm with the intention of assisting P to burgle the premises of D's employer.

---

[72] *Du Cros v Lambourne* [1907] 1 KB 40; *Tuck v Robson* [1970] 1 WLR 741 where a publican permitted customers to consume alcohol on the licensed premises outside the permitted hours; *JF Alford Transport* [1997] 2 Cr App R 326 where a company did nothing to prevent its employees falsifying their tachograph records; *Gaunt* [2003] EWCA Crim 3925.

[73] It is true that previously the Commission has taken the view that there is such a general principle – clause 27(3) of the Draft Criminal Code Bill and commentary in A Criminal Code for England and Wales, vol 2 Commentary on Draft Criminal Code Bill (1989) Law Com No 177 para 9.22. See Professor Glanville Williams, "Which of you did it?" (1989) 52 *Modern Law Review* 179 and, by the same author, "What should the Code do about Omissions?" (1987) 7 *Legal Studies* 92.

[74] Paras 4.69 to 4.74.

[75] Para 4.158.

5.63 It would be for the trial judge to rule whether D was under a duty. The question whether D had failed to discharge his or her duty would be one of fact. However, we would not wish to see D being criminally liable for *any* failure to take steps to discharge the duty. We believe that such a strict rule could operate harshly and lead to injustice. Instead, the test should be whether D failed to take reasonable steps to discharge the duty.[76]

Example 5P

D lives in her own property with her two children P aged 16 and V aged 15. P has never been violent towards V but on the night in question suddenly starts to assault V. P is of muscular build while D is diminutive in stature. D goes to the phone to call the police but P tears the phone from her and hits her with it. P continues to assault V.[77]

D has a duty to protect V. It would be for the prosecution to prove that she had failed to take reasonable steps to discharge that duty.

5.64 In cases where it was D's intention that the principal offence should be committed, it is difficult to envisage that D might nevertheless have taken reasonable steps to discharge his or her duty. However, we think that an exceptional case might arise where D, despite intending the commission of the principal offence, might legitimately claim that he or she had taken reasonable steps.

5.65 **We recommend that doing an act capable of encouraging or assisting a person to do a criminal act should include doing so by failing to take reasonable steps to discharge a duty.**

Failure to assist a constable to prevent a breach of the peace

5.66 At common law every citizen is under a duty to respond to a constable's request for assistance to prevent a breach of the peace.[78] We would not wish, and we do not believe that it would be thought to be either desirable or acceptable, for citizens to incur inchoate liability for merely failing to respond to such a request.

5.67 **We recommend that a person failing to respond to a constable's request for assistance in preventing a breach of the peace should not be regarded as the doing of an act capable of encouraging or assisting a person to do a criminal act.**

---

[76] Clause 15(2) of the Bill.

[77] Since P's assault on V was sudden and out of character, D cannot be liable for failing to prevent the initial assault. However, under our scheme the "doing of a criminal act" includes the continuation of a criminal act that has already began – cl 17(3)(a). Accordingly, the issue is whether D has failed to take reasonable steps to prevent the continuation of the assault.

[78] *Brown* (1841) Car & M 314, 174 ER 522.

Failure to exercise an entitlement to prevent or control the actions of P

5.68 We believe that it would be an over-extension of the criminal law if D could be inchoately liable on the basis that he or she had refrained from exercising an entitlement to prevent or control P's actions. Again, we emphasise that the new offences are inchoate offences capable of being committed even if the principal offence is not committed.

5.69 Every citizen is entitled to use reasonable force to control the actions of P in order to prevent P committing an offence.[79] We do not think it would be thought acceptable if D could be criminally liable for encouraging or assisting P to commit a crime merely because D failed to take action to prevent P committing the crime.

5.70 The entitlement that everyone has to control the actions of others in order to prevent the commission of an offence is an illustration of a general power. In addition, D may have a specific entitlement to control P's activities regardless of whether P is committing or is about to commit an offence, for example the owner of land is entitled to control the actions of others on the land:

Example 5Q

D, who has a telephone and a guard dog, is awoken by a noise coming from his garden. Opening the window, D asks P what he is doing. P replies "go back to bed". D, although believing that P is about to commit an assault on V, goes back to bed. P, encouraged by D's non-intervention, proceeds to assault V.

It might be thought that D's conduct is callous and displays a lack of empathy for V. In itself, this is not to justify the imposition of criminal liability. In this kind of example, if D could be made criminally liable for his failure to intervene, it would be a case of imposing liability because D was not being a good samaritan or "busy body". That is potentially far too harsh a consequence in such cases of non-intervention.[80]

The fault element

Introduction

5.71 We now consider what the fault element of the new offences should be. In addressing this issue, we emphasise that those who commit inchoate offences are punished because their conduct enhances the prospect of a principal offence being committed. Whether the principal offence is subsequently committed is irrelevant. Further, there is no correlation between the likelihood of the offence being committed and the strength of D's conviction that it will be committed:

---

[79] Criminal Law Act 1967, s 3.

[80] See the discussion in Simester and Sullivan, *Criminal Law Theory and Doctrine* (2nd ed 2003) pp 73 to 74.

> **Example 5R**
>
> D lends his car to P, knowing that P is disqualified from driving. D is sure that P will drive the car. However, it was always P's intention that X, P's wife who is not disqualified, should drive the car. In the event, X drives D's car.

On one view, it would be unduly intrusive and wasteful of resources for the criminal law to intervene where P had no intention of committing an offence. On the other view, the fact that P has not committed the offence of driving while disqualified, and never intended to, ought to make no difference to whether D is criminally liable. This is because when lending the car, D believed that P would use the car and, by doing so, would commit an offence. Assuming that there is merit in the latter view, does it follow that D should also be criminally liable if, for example, he or she merely suspected that P *might* use the car to commit an offence?

5.72   We have explained that the conduct element of the new offences is doing an act capable of encouraging or assisting the doing of a criminal act and that, in most cases, "criminal act" will have a restricted meaning, namely the conduct element of the principal offence.[81] However, the principal offence may also consist of a circumstance or consequence element, or both. So, we need to consider what the fault elements of the new offences should be in relation to not only the criminal act but also the circumstance and consequence elements, if any, of the principal offence.

D's fault in relation to the commission of the criminal act

5.73   The Supreme Court of Canada has recently considered this issue in the context of section 464(a) of the Canadian Criminal Code. The provision makes it an offence to "counsel another person to commit an indictable offence". The majority held that D must either intend that the principal offence be committed or knowingly counsel its commission while aware of the unjustified risk that it was likely to be committed. According to the majority, D can intend that the principal offence be committed even if the motive for counselling P to commit the offence is to make a financial profit.

---

[81]   Paras 5.23 to 5.26 above.

5.74 The view of the minority was that nothing less than an intention to persuade P to commit the offence should suffice. The minority felt that there was no distinction between intending to persuade P to commit the offence and intending that it should be committed. Charron J, delivering the reasons of the minority, said, "It is logical to infer that the counsellor who intends to persuade the person counselled to commit an offence intends that the offence be committed."[82] According to Charron J, the motive of D was "a piece of circumstantial evidence that may assist in determining an accused's state of mind". Underlying the opinion of the minority was a desire to ensure that the scope of the offence remained within the justifiable limits of the criminal law. The minority thought it essential to limit the scope of the offence in order to protect freedom of expression.

THE PROPOSALS IN THE CP

5.75 In the CP, the Commission provisionally proposed that D should incur liability for the offence of encouraging crime only if it was D's purpose[83] that another person should commit the principal offence.[84] The Commission thought that a narrow fault element was necessary because in many cases D's encouragement would do no more than embolden or fortify a person who had already decided to commit the principal offence. The Commission expressed concern that, unless purpose was required, D would incur liability for "the unlooked-for outcome of his comments on a matter of public interest".[85]

5.76 With regard to the offence of assisting crime, the Commission invited comment on whether the offence should be restricted to cases where it was D's purpose that the principal offence should be committed or whether the basis of liability should be broadened and, if so, how.[86]

5.77 The Commission said that *if* the fault element of assisting crime were to be broader than purpose that the principal offence be committed, the test would need to be defined with care.[87] It thought that were the test to be formulated in terms of "awareness", D should have to know or believe that P "is using or will use the assistance in the commission of a crime".[88] The Commission said:

---

[82] In the overwhelming majority of cases, this will be true. However, for an example of where D intends that P should be encouraged to commit an offence while being indifferent as to whether the offence is ultimately committed, see Appendix A para A.27.

[83] In the CP, the Commission employed "purpose" rather than "intention". By "purpose" the Commission meant acting with the aim and object of bringing about the commission of the principal offence. The Bill that accompanies this report uses intention rather than purpose.

[84] Para 4.154.

[85] Above. The Commission provided examples, one of which was D publishing an article criticising the use of animal experiments. The article inspires P to cause criminal damage to a laboratory.

[86] Para 4.95.

[87] Para 4.82.

[88] Para 4.83.

We consider that the law would be too broad if it were formulated in terms of … suspicion as to the principal's intentions. That consideration is particularly relevant to supply of assistance "in the ordinary course of business": for instance, the sale of a screwdriver or the provision of a taxi ride to a person known or thought to be a professional burglar. In such a case, D may well legitimately suspect that P will use the assistance given to him in one of his burglaries; but it seems too restrictive of ordinary activities to make supply criminal on the basis simply of suspicion of the use to which the supply is put.[89]

RESPONSES TO THE PROPOSALS IN THE CP

5.78 Only three respondents favoured restricting liability for assisting crime to cases where it was D's purpose that the principal offence be committed. The other respondents who addressed the issue favoured a test of knowledge or belief on D's part that another person is doing or will do acts that involve the commission of the principal offence.

IDENTIFYING THE APPROPRIATE FAULT ELEMENT

5.79 We no longer believe that there should be a different fault element for encouraging, on the one hand, and assisting, on the other. As we indicated above,[90] we no longer believe that encouraging and assisting are necessarily separate activities. In some cases they will overlap. If there were to be different fault elements, a potentially troublesome and unnecessary distinction would arise which would give rise to problems of charging and would be a recipe for legal argument at trial.

5.80 In addition, we no longer believe that liability for encouraging should be restricted to cases where it was D's purpose that the principal offence be committed. In the CP, the Commission thought that a narrow purpose test was necessary in order to ensure that D would not be liable for "the unlooked-for outcome" of comments on matters of public interest.[91] We think that the word expression "unlooked-for" is not free from ambiguity. If it means "uncontemplated", we agree that D should not be liable. If it means "undesired", we do not agree that the mere fact that D does not desire the commission of the principal offence should be a reason for exonerating D:

> **Example 5RR**
>
> D publishes a leaflet that contains the name and address of V, a convicted paedophile. D's intention is to encourage V to leave the neighbourhood. D also believes that the leaflet will encourage someone to assault V.

We see no reason why, in example 5RR, D should avoid liability *merely* because D's intention was not that V should be attacked but that V should be frightened into leaving the neighbourhood.

---

[89] Para 4.82.

[90] Para 5.20 above.

[91] Para 4.154.

5.81   We recognise that extending liability beyond cases where it is D's intention that the conduct element of the principal offence should be committed, raises the spectre of D incurring criminal liability for ostensibly lawful acts. A protestor may believe that his or her lawful protest will encourage the commission of retaliatory criminal conduct by others. Authors, journalists and publishers may believe that material which highlights what some would consider to be cruel or barbaric practices will encourage others to commit offences against those carrying out the practices:

Example 5S

D publishes an article that identifies a laboratory that uses animals in scientific experiments. D's intention is to persuade the laboratory to cease its activities. D believes that the article will encourage others to cause damage to the laboratory.

Example 5S

D is part of a television crew reporting at the scene of a riot. D's presence encourages the rioters to intensify their riotous behaviour. D is fully aware of the effect that the presence of the crew is having on the rioters.

We would not wish defendants in the position of D in examples 5S and 5SS to be convicted simply because they believe that their conduct will encourage others to commit offences. However, we believe that the answer is not by way of the inflexible and narrow test of liability proposed in the CP but by recourse to more context sensitive mechanisms.

5.82   Activities such as reporting, writing, publishing and protesting engage Articles 9, 10 and 11 of the European Convention on Human Rights and Fundamental Freedoms. The rights contained in those Articles are not absolute and may be restricted to the extent necessary for, amongst other things, the prevention of crime and disorder. We envisage that some prosecutions for the new offences will engage the relevant Articles.

5.83   The Bill accompanying this report does not contain any provisions in relation to Convention issues. This is because the Human Rights Act 1998 already brings the Convention rights into play. Since the rights under Articles 9, 10 and 11 are not absolute, cases will turn on their individual facts. The issue will be whether charging D with encouraging or assisting the commission of an offence engages D's rights under Articles 9, 10 and 11 and, if so, whether, on the facts, convicting D would be a disproportionate response in all the circumstances of the case.

5.84   In addition, in Part 6 we explain that, in cases where D's potential liability is based not on an intention but on a belief that a criminal act will be done, there should be a defence of acting reasonably in the circumstances.[92] In example 5S and 5SS, it would be open to D to claim that he or she had acted reasonably in the circumstances.

---

[92] See Part 6 paras 6.18 to 6.26 below.

5.85   As with encouraging, we do not believe that liability for assisting should be restricted to cases where it was D's intention that the criminal act be committed. If D's liability were so limited, it would necessarily exclude cases where D believes that a criminal act will be done with his or her assistance. It would mean that those who, purely for financial gain, supply articles, services or information believing that they will be used to commit a criminal act would incur no criminal liability. As the Commission stated in the CP:

> It is far from obvious that that outcome is correct, either from the point of view of justice or from the point of view of social protection. It might well be thought that those who willingly and knowingly assist in crime should be liable to punishment, not least as some means of impeding the commission of crimes that they would otherwise assist in; and that they act for profit should hardly be a reason for excusing them.[93]

5.86   However, as we noted above, inchoate liability for encouraging or assisting the commission of an offence has the potential to cast a very wide net of criminal liability, not least because liability is not dependent on the commission of any offence. Accordingly, there is a need for caution in determining the appropriate fault element. Referring to inchoate offences, Professor Ashworth has observed:

> … as the form of criminal liability moves further away from the infliction of harm, so the grounds of liability should become more narrow.[94]

5.87   If the fault element for encouraging or assisting crime is too broadly defined, consisting of no more than belief that a criminal act *might* be committed, there is a danger of deterring and unduly restricting ordinary trading, employment and social activities:

Example 5T

D owns a chemist's shop. P comes in and buys some lubricant jelly. D's understanding from (mistaken) local gossip is that P is a paedophile. D believes that P might use the jelly to commit an indecent assault on a child. D shares his belief with the next customer who reports what D has done to the police. They investigate and discover that P is a paediatrician. Local gossip has confused paedophile and paediatrician.

We do not believe that traders, such as D, ought to be liable merely because they believe that in selling their products they might be assisting the commission of a criminal act, particularly when, as in example 5T, there was never any possibility that the criminal act would be committed.

---

[93]   Para 4.86.

[94]   *Principles of Criminal Law* (4th ed 2003) p 425.

CONCLUSIONS AND RECOMMENDATIONS

5.88 We conclude, therefore, that to confine inchoate liability for encouraging or assisting to cases where it was D's intention that a criminal act should be committed would be unduly restrictive. Equally, it would be inappropriate to extend liability to include cases where D's belief was no more than that a criminal act might be committed.

5.89 **Accordingly, we recommend that in relation to the criminal act of the principal offence, D:**

    (1)   **in order to be guilty of the clause 1 offence, must intend[95] that the criminal act should be done or that a person be encouraged or assisted to do it;[96]**

    (2)   **in order to be guilty of the clause 2(1) offence, D, although not having to intend that the criminal act should be done, must believe that the criminal act will be done[97] and that his or her own act will encourage or assist the doing of the criminal act.[98]**

    D's state of mind where his or her conduct is capable of encouraging or assisting more than one criminal act[99]

5.90 In Part 4,[100] we said that some respondents to the CP had concerns about the desirability of an inchoate offence of assisting crime because of a perceived danger that it would result in an offence characterised by vagueness and uncertainty.

5.91 The danger that they were referring to is apparent in cases where D's conduct has the capacity to provide P with encouragement or assistance in relation to a range of possible criminal acts:

Example 5TT

D provides P with V's name and address. D correctly believes that P, using the information, will murder V or commit robbery against V or burgle V's premises. However, D is not sure which of those offences P will commit. P is arrested before being able to commit any of the offences.

As D believes that P will commit at least one of three criminal acts but is unsure which one(s) it will be, P's state of mind in relation to each criminal act within the range is something less than a belief that it will be committed.

---

[95] In the sense of what is usually referred to as "direct" intention. See clause 18 of the Bill and Appendix A paras A.26 to A.30 and para A.100.

[96] Clause 1(1)(b) of the Bill.

[97] Clause 2(1)(b)(i) of the Bill. Clause 3(5) of the Bill provides that it is sufficient that D believes that the criminal act will be done if certain conditions are met.

[98] Clause 2(1)(b)(ii) of the Bill.

[99] The relevant provisions in the Bill are clauses 2(2) and clause 3(2) to (7). For explanation, see Appendix A paras A.52 to A.55.

[100] See paras 4.15 to 4.16 above.

5.92 We have recommended that in order to be liable for the clause 2(1) offence, D must believe that his or her conduct will encourage or assist the commission of the criminal act of the principal offence and that P will do the criminal act.[101] We believe that it would not be inconsistent to also recommend that, if D's conduct is capable of encouraging or assisting the doing of a number of criminal acts, it should suffice if D believes that at least one of them will be committed. If D believes that one or more of a range of criminal acts will be committed, D's belief is more than merely a belief that P might commit a criminal act. In example 5TT, D believes that:

(1) if P does not commit murder or robbery, P will commit burglary;

(2) if P does not commit murder or burglary, P will commit robbery; and

(3) if P does not commit burglary or robbery, P will commit murder.

5.93 We believe that our approach is a principled one. If D does an act capable of encouraging or assisting P to commit criminal acts x, y and z, believing that P will commit at least one of them, D has no cause for complaint if he or she is prosecuted for encouraging or assisting one of those criminal acts.

5.94 **We recommend that, if D does an act capable of encouraging or assisting the doing of one or more of a number of criminal acts, D must believe:**

(1) **that at least one of those acts will be done but without having any belief as to which it will be;[102] and**

(2) **that his or her conduct will encourage or assist the doing of at least one of those acts.[103]**

5.95 However, since D's state of mind in relation to each criminal act is something less than a belief that it will be committed, we think that it ought to be possible to prosecute D for only one offence. It will be for the Crown Prosecution Service to decide the criminal act on which to base the prosecution of D. They may be minded to choose the one which they believe provides the best chance of securing a conviction, even if it is not the most serious.

5.96 **We recommend that if D does an act capable of encouraging or assisting the doing of one or more of a number of criminal acts and D believes:**

(1) **that at least one of a number of criminal acts will be done but has no belief as to which it will be; and**

(2) **that his or her act will encourage or assist the doing of at least one of those criminal acts**

D may be prosecuted for only one offence.[104]

---

[101] Para 5.89(2) above.

[102] Clause 2(2)(b)(i) of the Bill. Clause 3(6) of the Bill provides that it is sufficient if D believes that one or more of the criminal acts will be done if certain conditions are met.

[103] Clause 2(2)(b)(ii) of the Bill.

5.97 In example 5TT, D believed that P would commit a criminal act but could not identify which one it would be. By contrast:

> **Example 5U**
>
> D wants to intimidate V who owes D money. D says to his henchman, P, "Go round to V's house and smash the place up *and* when you have done that either steal something valuable *or* rough V up a bit. Make sure he gets the message". Before he can go to V's house, the police arrest P. P tells the police what D told him to do.

In this example, D believes that P will commit a criminal act, smashing up V's property and, in addition, believes that P will commit another criminal act but does not know whether it will be appropriating property or physically attacking V.

5.98 We believe that it ought to be possible to prosecute D both in relation to the criminal act of smashing up V's furniture and either for the criminal act of appropriating property or for the criminal act of physically attacking V.[105]

5.99 A more problematic situation is where D believes that P will commit a particular criminal act (*x*) and also *might* commit an additional criminal act (*y*):

> **Example 5UU**
>
> D is annoyed by the alarm on V's car going off. D gives P a hammer and tells P to go and silence the vehicle. D, realising that P might also use the hammer to assault V, tells P not to approach the car if V is there. An off-duty policeman hears the conversation.

We think that to permit the prosecution of D for an inchoate offence of encouraging or assisting assault when D's state of mind is a mere belief that P might assault V would represent a significant and unwarranted departure from our general position. It would constitute an over-extension of criminal liability. It would be different if, similar to example 5U, D believed that, in addition to committing criminal damage, P *will* either assault V or rob V but is unsure which offence P will commit.

D's state of mind as to the mens rea of P in doing the criminal act

5.100 D ought not to incur liability merely because D intends or believes that P should or will commit an "act" that is criminal. The "act" that is criminal in theft is the appropriation of property. It would be absurd if D could be criminally liable for doing nothing more than encouraging P to do that act:

---

[104] Clause 3(4) of the Bill. If, however, D *intends* that a number of criminal acts should be committed, it will be possible to prosecute D for the clause 1 offence in relation to each criminal act even if D did not believe that all of them would be committed – clause 3(1) of the Bill.

[105] Clause 3(3) of the Bill and Appendix A para A.53.

Example 5V

At P's request, D keeps watch outside a house belonging to V. P tells D that he is going to enter the house to retrieve goods which P says belong to him. In fact, the goods belong to V. It was P's intention to take them and sell them to fund his drug habit. P abandons the project when, on arriving at the house, it appears that V is at home.

D should not be liable for encouraging or assisting burglary or theft even though it was P's intention, unknown to D, to sell the goods.

5.101 However, conversely, in some cases it is D, not P, who would satisfy the fault element of the principal offence were the criminal act to be done:

Example 5VV

D, at P's request, keeps watch on V's house. D believes that P is going to steal property from the house. In fact, P intends to take property that he believes belongs to him. Before P can even attempt to enter the house, V returns. P abandons the enterprise.

Example 5X

D encourages P, aged 8, to punch V.

Example 5XX

D encourages P to steal some books from the library and says that, if P does not do so, D will inflict serious harm on P's child.

In example 5VV, were P to enter V's house and take the goods, P would not commit burglary[106] because he honestly believed that he was the owner of the goods.[107] In example 5X, P is under the age of criminal responsibility.[108] In example 5XX, P will be able to plead duress as a complete defence.[109] However, in each example, D has encouraged or assisted the commission of a criminal act which, were he to do it, he would do so with the state of mind to be convicted of the principal offence.

---

[106] Contrary to the Theft Act 1968, s 9(1)(b).

[107] Theft Act 1968, s 2(1)(a).

[108] Children and Young Persons Act 1933, s 50.

[109] *Bourne* (1952) 36 Cr App R 125.

5.102 In Part 3,[110] we explained that under the present law it is uncertain whether D can be convicted of incitement if D incites P to do an act which, if done by P, would result in P not committing any offence. Under our recommendations there will be no uncertainty.

5.103 We do not believe D ought to be exonerated merely because it would not be possible to convict P of the principal offence were he or she to do the criminal act. Instead, the focus should be on D's state of mind. In principle, it ought to be possible to convict D if D's state of mind is such that, were he or she to do the criminal act, he or she would do it with the fault required for conviction of the principal offence.

5.104 In some cases, D will be incapable of doing the criminal act, for example a woman cannot do the criminal act of rape – penetration "with the penis".[111] However, D ought not to escape liability merely by virtue of being incapable of doing the criminal act. If D, a woman, encourages P to penetrate V with his penis believing that, were P to do so, it would be without the consent of V,[112] it ought to be possible to convict D encouraging or assisting rape even if P would not be guilty of rape because of a reasonable belief that V would consent.[113]

5.105 **We recommend that, in order for D to be convicted of the clause 1 or a clause 2 offence:**

    (1) D must believe that, were another person to do the criminal act, that person would do it with the fault required for conviction of the principal offence;[114] or

    (2) D's state of mind must be such that, were he or she to do the criminal act, he or she would do it with that fault.[115] D is to be assumed to be able to do the criminal act in question.[116]

The circumstance and consequence elements, if any, of the principal offence

5.106 In the previous section, we said that, in order to be liable, D must have one of two states of mind. D must either believe that were another person to do the criminal act, that person would do it with the fault required for conviction of the principal offence or D's own state of mind is such that, were he to do it, he would do it with that fault. However, some offences can be committed without the principal offender having to be at fault in relation to the consequence or circumstance element. In this section, we consider D's liability for encouraging or assisting the commission of such offences.

---

[110] Paras 3.26 to 3.32.

[111] Sexual Offences Act 2003, s 1(1)(a).

[112] Sexual Offences Act 2003, s 1(1)(b).

[113] Sexual Offences Act 2003, s 1(1)(c).

[114] Clauses 1(2)(a) and 2(3)(a) of the Bill.

[115] Clauses 1(2)(b) and 2(3)(b) of the Bill.

[116] Clause 11 of the Bill.

CONSEQUENCES

The correspondence principle

5.107   In relation to principal offenders, Ashworth and Campbell have highlighted the importance of what they refer to as the correspondence principle:

> If the offence is defined in terms of certain consequences and certain circumstances, the mental element ought to correspond with that by referring to those consequences or circumstances. If a mental element as to a lesser consequence were acceptable, this would amount to constructive criminal liability.[117]

5.108   The correspondence principle is not in fact an accurate descriptive generalisation of offences. This is because many offences that have a consequence element do not require that a principal offender be at fault in relation to the defined consequence. The law of offences against the person is replete with examples. Section 20 of the Offences against the Person Act 1861 makes it an offence to maliciously wound or to inflict grievous bodily harm. However, the offence can be committed if the accused merely foresaw that his or her conduct might result in *some* physical harm.[118] A person can be convicted of murder even though he or she did not intend to kill but merely intended to cause really serious harm. If a person commits an offence that creates a reasonably foreseeable risk of causing some, albeit minor, harm to V, he or she is guilty of manslaughter if in fact V dies. The risk of death does not even have to be reasonably foreseeable.[119] These are all constructive liability offences - the requisite fault element does not have to correspond to the consequence defined by the offence but only to a lesser consequence.

CIRCUMSTANCES

Strict Liability

5.109   A principal offender can also be guilty of some offences that have a circumstance element without being at fault in relation to the circumstance. The circumstance element of the offence of driving while disqualified[120] is being disqualified from holding or obtaining a driving licence. The offence is committed irrespective of whether the accused is aware that he or she is so disqualified.[121] Section 5 of the Sexual Offences Act 2003 makes it an offence to rape a child who is under 13. A person can be convicted of the offence even if he or she reasonably believes that the child is aged 13 or over.[122] These are strict liability offences because whether or not the principal offender is at fault in relation to the circumstance element is irrelevant to the issue of liability.

---

[117] "Recklessness in Assault – And in General?" (1991) 107 *Law Quarterly Review* 187, 192.

[118] *Mowatt* [1968] 1 QB 421.

[119] *Church* [1966] 1 QB 59; *DPP v Newbury* [1977] AC 500

[120] Contrary to Road Traffic Act 1988, s 103.

[121] *Bowsher* [1973] RTR 202; *Miller* [1975] 2 All ER 974. A court may in certain circumstances disqualify a person from holding or obtaining a driving licence even though that person is not physically before the court.

[122] As confirmed in *R v G* [2006] EWCA Crim 819.

IMPLICATIONS FOR THE NEW OFFENCES THAT WE ARE RECOMMENDING

5.110   It might be thought that if the principal offence that D is encouraging or assisting is a constructive or strict liability offence, D's fault should merely have to mirror that of the principal offender. However, it has to be remembered that D's liability is inchoate. D is liable not for committing a principal offence but for encouraging or assisting the commission of a principal offence which in fact may never be committed:

> **Example 5Y**
>
> D asks P to drive D's wife, who is in labour, to the local hospital. P says that he is too busy, However, D offers to pay P £100 and P agrees to do so. P is unaware that the previous day, a court had disqualified him from holding or obtaining a driving licence. Likewise, D is unaware that P has been disqualified. Just as P is about to leave to drive D's wife to the hospital, an ambulance arrives and takes D's wife to hospital.

If P had driven D's wife to hospital, he, despite being unaware that he was disqualified, would have committed the offence of driving while disqualified because it is a strict liability offence.

5.111   We believe that the law would be too severe if, in example 5Y, D could be convicted of encouraging or assisting the offence of driving while disqualified. We acknowledge that it might be thought that this treats D more favourably than the prospective principal offender, P. However, as a general rule, P is in a better position to appreciate the nature of the risk that he is taking in committing the conduct element.[123]

5.112   Accordingly, we believe that for all offences that include a circumstance or consequence element, or both, D must be at fault in relation to the consequence or circumstance even if the offence is a constructive or strict liability offence. However, to say that D must be at fault in relation to those elements leaves unanswered the question: what is meant by "fault"?

[123] In example 5Y, P can hardly complain. He would have been notified by the court that the court was considering disqualifying him and he would have had the opportunity to attend court to make representations as to why he should not be disqualified – Magistrates' Courts Act 1980, s 11(4).

THE MEANING OF FAULT IN RELATION TO CIRCUMSTANCES AND CONSEQUENCES

Substantive offences

5.113   The criminal law recognises numerous fault elements. They include intention, recklessness, maliciousness, negligence, knowledge, belief and suspicion. Different principal offences have different fault elements. Most offences require that the principal offender must deliberately, as opposed to inadvertently, commit the proscribed conduct. However, there is a great deal of variation when it comes to the circumstance and consequence elements. In order to be convicted of some offences, the principal offender must intend to bring about the proscribed consequence.[124] However, for other offences it suffices if he or she foresaw a risk that the consequence would occur.[125] Some offences require that the principal offender perpetrates the proscribed conduct knowing or believing that he or she is doing so in the circumstances defined by the offence.[126] For other offences, it suffices if the principal offender perpetrates the proscribed conduct while aware of a risk that he or she is doing so in those circumstances.[127]

Inchoate offences

5.114   Until comparatively recently, the inchoate offences of attempt, conspiracy and incitement have required a high degree of fault on the part of an accused in relation to all the elements of the principal offence. If D and P conspire to commit a principal offence that has a circumstance element, they must each "*intend or know* that that … circumstance shall or will exist at the time when the conduct constituting the principal offence is to take place".[128] The House of Lords has confirmed that D and P must intend or know that the circumstance shall or will exist even though each could be convicted of committing the principal offence if they merely suspected that the circumstance element of the offence was satisfied.[129]

5.115   By contrast, in the context of attempt, the courts have diluted the requisite fault element. In *Khan*[130] the Court of Appeal held that recklessness as to the circumstance element sufficed. In *Attorney-General's Reference (No 3 of 1992)*[131] the Court of Appeal by implication held that that recklessness as to the consequence element can ground liability in certain cases.

---

[124] Eg, causing grievous bodily harm with intent contrary to Offences against the Person Act, s 18.

[125] Eg, the offence of criminal damage contrary to Criminal Damage Act 1971, s 1(1) - G [2003] UKHL 50; [2004] 1 AC 1034

[126] Eg, the offence of dishonest handling contrary to the Theft Act, s 22 (1).

[127] Eg, the offence of criminal damage contrary to the Criminal Damage Act 1971, s 1(1).

[128] Criminal Law Act 1977, s 1(2).

[129] *Saik* [2006] UKHL 18; [2006] 2 WLR 993.

[130] [1990] 2 All ER 783. In so holding, the Court of Appeal reflected cl 49(2) of the Law Commission's Draft Criminal Code.

[131] (1993) 98 Cr App R 383.

5.116   Whatever the merits of the current law in relation to conspiracy and attempt, we believe that there are important differences between attempt and conspiracy, on the one hand, and encouraging or assisting crime, on the other. When D1 and D2 conspire to commit an offence, they agree on a joint criminal enterprise. Together, they engage in conduct that is, as in the case of an attempt to commit a crime, designed to lead eventually to the commission of an offence. By way of contrast, in the case of encouraging or assisting crime, D's own conduct relates to the separate conduct of another person who is to commit the offence. That conduct is not agreed upon and does not necessarily involve D's future participation.

5.117   Therefore, there is a sense in which liability for encouraging or assisting crime is at least "twice removed" from the commission of the crime itself. It is inchoate liability in that the principal offence need not be committed but, by way of contrast with conspiracy and attempt, it also necessarily relates to the separate conduct of another person. The fact that offences of encouraging or assisting crime are "twice removed" from the commission of the principal offence is what makes an uncompromisingly narrow fault element essential.

CONCLUSIONS AND RECOMMENDATIONS

5.118   **We recommend that if, in addition to a criminal act, a circumstance element or a consequence element, or both, must be proved for conviction of the principal offence, D, in order to be convicted of the clause 1 or a clause 2 offence:**

   (1)   **must intend that the criminal act be done in those circumstances or with those consequences;[132] or**

   (2)   **must believe that, were the criminal act to be done, it would be done in those circumstances or with those consequences.[133]**

5.119   The following example illustrates how the recommendations would apply:

> **Example 5YY**
>
> In return for payment, D lends P a baseball bat believing that P is going to use it to inflict minor bodily harm on V. P uses the bat to attack V and intentionally kills V.

D is guilty of encouraging or assisting the commission of assault occasion actual bodily harm.[134] D is not guilty of encouraging or assisting murder because D did not believe that the criminal act of hitting V with the bat would result in the death of V.

---

[132] Clause 1(3)(a) of the Bill. For explanation, see Appendix A paras A.31 to A.44.

[133] Clauses 1(3)(b) and 2(4) of the Bill. For explanation, see Appendix A paras A.45 to A.51.

[134] Contrary to the Offences against the Person Act 1861, s 47.

5.120   If, in example 5YY, D believed that the criminal act would result in *serious* but not lethal harm to V, D would not be guilty of encouraging or assisting murder. Instead, D would be guilty either of encouraging or assisting the offence of causing grievous bodily harm with intent[135] or of encouraging or assisting the offence of unlawfully and maliciously inflicting grievous bodily harm.[136] Which of the two offences D would be guilty of encouraging or assisting would depend on whether or not D believed that P would attack V intending to cause grievous bodily harm.

5.121   It is important to note that, although in order to be convicted of the clause 1 offence, D must intend that the criminal act be done, D does not have to intend that it be done in the circumstances or with the consequences defined by the principal offence. D has merely to believe that it will be done in the circumstances or with the consequences:

Example 5Z

D, knowing that his son P is in debt to Z, urges P to commit a burglary in order to clear the debt. D advises P to take a cosh and to hit the security guard at the premises, V, over the head. D's intention is that V should be incapacitated but not that V should suffer any harm. However, D believes that V will suffer injury, albeit not serious. While on way to commit the burglary, P is stopped by the police and searched. P tells the police what D had told him to do.

D's intention was that the criminal act should be done. In addition, D believed that, as a result of the criminal act being done, V would suffer bodily harm. D has committed the offence of intentionally encouraging or assisting the commission of the offence of assault occasioning actual bodily harm.

Conditional intents and beliefs with regard to circumstances

5.122   At this point, we must address a possible complication:

Example 5ZZ

D gives P some money to give to V to persuade V to loan his car to D and P for the afternoon. D says to P "if V is prepared to loan the car, all well and good. If V will not lend it to you, just take it".

In this example, D's preference is for the car to be obtained legally but, if that is not possible, D wishes P to take it anyway.[137]

---

[135] Contrary to the Offences against the Person Act 1861, s 18.

[136] Contrary to the Offences against the Person Act 1861, s 20.

[137] In example 5ZZ, the principal offence is taking a motor vehicle without the consent of the owner contrary to the Theft Act 1968, s 12(1). The circumstance element of the offence is the lack of the owner's consent.

5.123   In example 5ZZ, D would prefer the vehicle to be obtained with V's consent but has told P that, if consent is not forthcoming, P should take it anyway. D's attitude is that of a person who is determined to have the use of V's car come what may. In as much as D envisages V's car being taken without V's consent, D could not care whether the circumstance element of the offence is or is not present.

5.124   We believe that D ought to be criminally liable if he or she is prepared for a criminal act to be done not caring whether or not the circumstances element of the offence is present. We believe that clauses 1(2)(a) and 2(3)(a) as drafted capture such cases. They require D to believe that if P were to do the criminal act P would do it with the necessary fault. This covers not only the situation where D believes that P will do the criminal act with the necessary fault but also the case where D believes that P will do the act with the necessary fault if P cannot do it fault free. The wording of clauses 1(2)(a) and 2(3)(a) includes the implicit conditional. The same analysis applies to clauses 1(3)(b) and 2(4).

5.125   We also believe that such cases are covered by clauses 1(2)(b) and 2(3)(b). Each clause is based upon the hypothetical situation of D doing that which he or she intended to encourage or assist P to do. If D encourages P to have sexual intercourse with V and to do so even if V does not consent, we believe that a jury would have little difficulty in concluding that D's state of mind was such that that he would have raped V if he were in P's shoes and V did not consent to intercourse.

5.126   As it is based on a hypothetical doing by D of that which he intended to encourage P to do, it matters not that D claims that he would never himself actually have done the criminal act in question. D encourages P to have sexual intercourse with V and to do so even if V does not consent. D does not mind if P rapes V but would never consider raping her himself. However, D will be liable because were he to have done what he intended to encourage P to do, he would have done it with the necessary fault element. He stands in the hypothetical shoes of P in the same way as he would if he had used an innocent P to commit the offence.

PENALTIES

5.127   **We recommend that for committing the clause 1 or a clause 2, D should be liable:**

(1)   **if the principal offence is murder, to imprisonment for life; and**

(2)   **in any other case, unless an enactment provides otherwise, to any penalty for which D would be liable on conviction of the principal offence.**[138]

MODE OF TRIAL

5.128   **We recommend that the mode of trial in the case of the clause 1 or a clause 2 offence should be determined as if D had been charged with the principal offence.**[139]

[138] Clause 12 of the Bill.

PART 6
DEFENCES AND EXEMPTIONS

INTRODUCTION

6.1 In this Part we consider defences and exemptions from liability. In the CP, the Commission's approach to defences and exemptions reflected the different fault elements of the two inchoate offences that it was proposing. The fault element for encouraging crime was intention that an offence should be committed whereas that for assisting crime was knowledge or belief that an offence would be committed.

6.2 Broadly, the Commission proposed that there should be no defences and exemptions available to persons whose intention was that the principal offence should be committed. It followed, therefore, that defences and exemptions were to be denied to those who encouraged the commission of an offence. By contrast, the Commission proposed that some defences and exemptions should be available to those who indifferently assisted the commission of an offence.

6.3 As will become apparent, we are no longer of the view that the availability of defences should depend on whether D provides encouragement as opposed to assistance. We begin by setting out those defences and exemptions that we recommend should be available. We then go on to set out our reasons for rejecting other defences that were highlighted for consideration in the CP.

DEFENCES AND EXEMPTIONS THAT WE ARE RECOMMENDING

Acting to prevent the commission of offences or to prevent or limit harm

6.4 In Part 3 we said[140] that there is uncertainty as to whether acting for the purposes of law enforcement can be a defence to preliminary offences such as incitement and conspiracy. Frustrating the commission of crime can take one of three forms:

(1) encouraging or assisting the commission of an offence but with the purpose of preventing its commission. An example would be where a police informer or undercover officer does something to encourage or assist the commission of a robbery but the purpose is to ensure that it is not committed;

(2) encouraging or assisting the commission of an offence not in order to prevent its commission but in order to reduce its harmful effects;[141]

---

[139] Clause 9 of the Bill.

[140] Paras 3.50 to 3.54.

[141] Clarke (1984) 80 Cr App R 344 is an illustration. D participated in a burglary but claimed to have done so in order to prevent the other participants escaping and to ensure that the property would be recovered.

(3)   encouraging the commission or attempted commission of an offence in order to prevent the commission of future offences, for example an undercover officer who acts in a way designed to encourage a hitherto undetected serial rapist to attack her.

The proposals in the CP

6.5   In the CP, the Commission proposed that there should be a defence of law enforcement to its proposed offence of assisting crime. It proposed that the defence should be available to any individual whose "overall course of conduct" was directed towards frustrating the commission of the principal offence.[142] The Commission invited comment on whether the defence should extend to incidental offences, for example a theft committed in order to obtain property to be used in a robbery.

Responses to the proposals in the CP

6.6   The majority of respondents who addressed the issue thought that there should be a defence of acting in order to prevent crime. Of the majority, some felt that the assister should be exonerated only for the offence that he or she intended to frustrate but not for an incidental offence. Some respondents expressed misgivings about the defence being available to private citizens.

6.7   One respondent, while accepting that the defence should be wide enough to exonerate those involved in undercover "sting" operations, such as test purchases and "manna from heaven" operations,[143] thought that a criterion of "reasonableness" should be built into the defence. Most respondents believed that D should bear the burden of proving the defence.

Conclusions

6.8   We believe that in principle there should be a defence of acting in order to prevent the commission of an offence or in order to prevent or limit harm. We do so for two reasons:

(1)   it is in the public interest that acts be done in order to prevent crime or to prevent or limit the occurrence of harm. Accordingly, an act of encouragement or assistance, the overall purpose of which is to prevent crime or to prevent or limit harm, is justified because of its value to society;

(2)   those whose overall purpose in encouraging or assisting the commission of an offence is to prevent crime or to prevent or limit harm are acting as good citizens and should not be punished for doing so;

---

[142] Para 4.125.

[143] An example of a test purchase is a child under the age of 16, and under the control of the local authority trading standards department, going into a shop and buying a lottery ticket. A "manna from heaven" operation is one where police, in the course of an investigation into suspected criminal behaviour, provide an opportunity for anybody to commit the criminal behaviour that they are investigating, eg the police expose cartons of cigarettes, apparently unguarded, in the back of a van parked in the street – *Williams v DPP* (1993) 98 Cr App R 209.

6.9　At one stage, we thought that the defence should only be available to formal and informal agents of the state - police and customs officers, local authority trading standards officers, agents working under their control and civilian informers subject to regulation and supervision by the relevant law enforcement authority. We thought that the arguments in favour of such a restriction were:

(1)　law enforcement is primarily the responsibility of the state. Private citizens and the media should be discouraged from participating in offences on their own initiative even if the motive is to prevent crime. Important considerations are the safety of the citizen, the dangers of private vendettas being pursued and private acts hindering the activities of the state's law enforcement agencies.

(2)　there should be external controls in order to ensure that D's involvement is proportionate to the overall aim of an operation to prevent crime;

(3)　to obviate the possibility of the defence being raised by criminals who might prepare the necessary groundwork for a false defence of crime prevention prior to and during their involvement in a criminal enterprise.

6.10　At the same time, we recognised that the defence would be open to abuse even if restricted to agents of the state. Test purchases can be made when there are no reasonable grounds for suspecting or believing that a trader is flouting the law. Police informers sometimes have their own agenda and it may sometimes be unclear whether their actions have been properly supervised and controlled.

6.11　In addition, we now believe that it would be exceedingly difficult to define exhaustively the persons who would be eligible to plead the defence. It is vital that the question of who can rely on the defence does not turn on technicalities. Accordingly, we are not recommending that the defence should be limited to particular individuals or categories.

SHOULD INCIDENTAL OFFENCES BE EXCLUDED FROM THE SCOPE OF THE DEFENCE?

6.12　We believe that the defence should exonerate D for encouraging or assisting *any* offence provided D's overall purpose was to prevent the commission of crime or to prevent harm and provided that D acted reasonably in the circumstances:

Example 6A

P is a member of a gang planning an armed robbery. D, who has infiltrated the gang, tells P where to steal a lorry which can be used in the robbery. D does so in order to maintain credibility with members of the gang. D's aim is to prevent the commission of the robbery.

Admittedly, D's assistance was not for the purpose of preventing P to commit theft. However, that ought not to preclude D pleading the defence to a charge of encouraging or assisting theft. D ought to be able to say that what he or she did was in order to frustrate the commission of another offence. The critical issue is the reasonableness of D's conduct. Was it reasonable in the circumstances to assist the commission of offence *x* in order to prevent the commission of offence *y*?

A REQUIREMENT OF ACTING REASONABLY

6.13 In the CP, the Commission said:

> ... it should be enough that [D] *believes* that his act of assistance is necessary as part of the implementation of his purpose of preventing the commission of the principal crime.[144]

However, we now believe that in order to rely on the defence, it must have been reasonable in the circumstances for D to have acted as he or she did.

6.14 This is to ensure that D can only successfully plead the defence if what D did was proportionate to the seriousness of the offence or harm that D was trying to prevent or limit. It is not in the public interest for D to encourage or assist the commission of an offence if the offence in question is more serious than the offence that D is seeking to prevent. In this regard, the requirement of reasonableness is a restraining principle and will operate as a curb on those who might think that any conduct is justifiable in the public interest. For example, the defence should not be available if D encourages P to shoot V when V is stealing some vegetables from P's allotment, even if D believes that it is necessary to shoot V in order to prevent V stealing the vegetables.

6.15 D should bear the legal burden of proving the defence on a balance of probabilities. We do not believe that placing the legal burden on D is incompatible with the presumption of innocence contained in Article 6(2) of the European Convention on Human Rights and Fundamental Freedoms. This is because the prosecution will still have had to prove the elements of the offence and if D raises the defence he or she is likely to be the only or the primary source of information as to his or her purpose.

Recommendation

6.16 **We recommend that it should be a defence to a charge under clause 1 or clause 2 if D proves that:**

> **(1)   he or she acted for the purpose of:**
>
> > **(a)   preventing the commission of either the offence that he or she was encouraging or assisting or another offence; or**
> >
> > **(b)   to prevent or limit the occurrence of harm;[145] and**

---

[144] Para 4.126 (emphasis added).

[145] Clause 4(1)(a) of the Bill. For explanation, see Appendix A paras A.57 to A.60.

(2)   it was reasonable to act as D did in the circumstances.[146]

Implications for conspiracy

6.17   It is beyond the scope of this report to make formal recommendations in relation to the inchoate offence of conspiracy. However, we think that it would be anomalous if there were a defence of crime prevention to encouraging or assisting the commission of an offence but not to conspiring to commit an offence. Accordingly, we suggest that consideration be given to reversing the decision of the Privy Council in *Yip Chiu-Cheung v R*[147] by way of a statutory defence of crime prevention in cases of conspiracy.

A defence of acting reasonably

6.18   We acknowledge that the clause 2(1) offence raises the spectre of D being liable for conduct consisting of normal and commonplace activities or, more broadly, activities that might be thought to be within D's rights to engage in:

Example 6B

D is driving at 70 miles per hour in the outside lane of a motorway. P, driving faster, comes up behind D. D pulls over to let P overtake.

D, although not intending that P should continue speeding, knows that pulling over will assist P to continue speeding.[148]

6.19   We believe that there should be a defence which will prevent D being held liable for acts which, in the circumstances, D could reasonably have expected to be able to engage in free from the taint of criminality. In other words, it ought to be open to D to say that his or her conduct was reasonable in the circumstances.

6.20   We are reinforced in this view by the fact that the criminal law has in other contexts recognised defences based on acceptable conduct, that is conduct that would, by virtue of its very ordinariness, not be regarded by most people as criminal. Thus, in the context of assault and battery, there is a defence of acceptable conduct that prevents D being criminally liable for assaulting P by clapping P on the back as a congratulatory gesture. D is not criminally liable because his or her conduct takes the form of "physical conduct which is generally acceptable in the ordinary conduct of daily life".[149]

---

[146] Clause 4(1)(b) of the Bill.

[147] [1995] 1 AC 111.

[148] For a further example, see example 1K in Part 1 para 1.31. Another example would be a person who locks his or her door to prevent V seeking refuge in D's house from a gang intent on assaulting V.

[149] *Collins v Wilcock* [1984] 1 WLR, 1172, 1174 by Lord Goff.

6.21   Another context is the Protection from Harassment Act 1997 ("the 1997 Act"). While harassment can be very serious, it may also take place in a context in which it is acceptable conduct, for example D continually asking his or her neighbour to turn down the volume of the music that the neighbour is constantly playing loudly. Accordingly, section 1(3)(c) of the 1997 Act provides that D is not guilty of harassment if "in the particular circumstances the pursuit of the conduct was reasonable".

6.22   A defence of acting reasonably in the circumstances would operate as a substantive and independent basis for acquittal. It would enable a jury to balance D's claim that he should be regarded as within his rights to act as he did against, amongst other things, the seriousness of the offence that D believes will occur as a result of providing the encouragement or assistance. It is true that the responses of different courts and juries on the issue of reasonableness may be unpredictable. However, we are not aware that similar defences have caused undue difficulties for juries and magistrates.

6.23   We acknowledge that a reasonableness defence has the potential for operating in an unfettered way. We would not wish the defence to result in unmeritorious acquittals. Accordingly, it should be a requirement of the defence that D acted reasonably in the circumstances that he or she knew or reasonably believed existed:

Example 6C

D and P, who are acquaintances, are at an inn in an area where there is no public transport. D has driven there and plans to stay overnight. P, who D knows is disqualified from driving, was driven there by X. After a row, X drives off. P approaches D and says that the inn has received a phone call from P's wife who is distraught because their child has been seriously injured in an accident. D asks P if D will drive P home. D says that he has had too much to drink, as P well knows, but reluctantly agrees to give P the keys to his car. Before P can drive off, he is spotted by policemen and arrested on another matter. P's wife had not rung the inn.

Under our recommendations, D must reasonably believe that P's child has been seriously injured and that P had no effective lawful means of getting home. In deciding whether the beliefs were reasonably held, a court would be entitled to take into account the measures that were available to D for verifying P's account and for concluding that there were no effective lawful means open to P for getting home. If the court found that D's beliefs were reasonably held, it would then have to consider whether, in the light of those beliefs, D acted reasonably in providing P with the means to drive while disqualified.

6.24   Unlike the defence of acting to prevent the commission of an offence or to prevent harm, we are not recommending that this defence should be available to if it was D's *intention* that P should commit an offence with D's encouragement or assistance.

6.25 As with the defence of acting to prevent the commission of an offence or to prevent harm, the burden of proof should be on D to prove all the elements of the defence on a balance of probabilities.[150]

Recommendation

6.26 **We recommend that it should be a defence to a charge under clause 2 if D proves that his or her conduct was reasonable in the circumstances as he knew or reasonably believed them to be.[151]**

An exemption from liability in cases of protective offences

The common law

6.27 In Part 1,[152] we referred to the common law *Tyrrell*[153] exemption. In *Tyrrell* P, an adult, had unlawful sexual intercourse with D, a child aged between 13 to 16.[154] It was alleged that D had encouraged P to commit the offence. It was held that D could not be convicted of committing the offence as an accessory *or of inciting the offence* because the offence had been enacted for the purpose of protecting a category of persons and D fell within the category. This was because the relevant statutory provision was "passed for the purpose of protecting young women and girls against themselves".[155] According to Lord Coleridge CJ, Parliament could not "have intended that the girls for whose protection [the offence] was passed should be punishable under it for the offences committed upon themselves".[156]

---

[150] Para 6.15 above.

[151] The defence is set out in cl 5 of the Bill. For explanation, see Appendix A paras A.61 to A.63.

[152] Para 1.33 above

[153] [1894] 1 QB 710.

[154] Contrary to the Criminal Law Amendment Act 1885, s 5.

[155] [1894] 1 QB 710, 712.

[156] Above.

6.28   This suggests that the underlying principle is that where the purpose of a statutory offence is to protect a category of persons, no member of that category can be convicted of committing the offence as a secondary party or of inciting its commission. The principle has been applied in the context of incest,[157] although it is arguable that the basis of the offence was eugenic rather than protectionist.[158] The principle has also been applied where D, a prostitute, was charged with being an accessory to her husband's offence of living on immoral earnings.[159] The offence existed in part to protect prostitutes but that was not its only function. An additional reason for the offence was to prevent fortunes being made by those who organise prostitution.

The Sexual Offences Act 2003

6.29   The Sexual Offences Act 2003 is largely silent on the *Tyrrell* exemption. The Act creates specific sexual offences designed to protect children under 13, namely rape of a child under 13,[160] assault of a child under 13 by penetration[161] and sexual assault of a child under 13.[162] Each offence can be committed by a child under 13.[163]

Example 6D

D, a girl aged 12, encourages P, a boy aged 12, to allow her to perform oral sex on him. P permits D to do this.

---

[157] *Whitehouse* [1977] QB 868; *Pickford* [1995] 1 Cr App R 420.

[158] Thus, the offence applied to sexual intercourse between adult brothers and sisters and to intercourse between fathers and adult daughters. See V. Bailey and S. Blackburn, "The Punishment of Incest Act 1908: A Case Study in Law Creation" [1979] *Criminal Law Review* 708; S. Wolfram "Eugenics and the Punishment of Incest Act 1908" [1983] *Criminal Law Review* 308.The offence of incest has been repealed by the Sexual Offences Act 2003. Instead, there are familial child sex offences (ss 25-29) and offences of sex with an adult relative (ss 64-65).

[159] Contrary to what was the Sexual Offences Act 1956, s 30.

[160] Section 5. The offence is committed if a person intentionally penetrates the vagina, anus or mouth of another with his penis. The offence is punishable by a maximum term of imprisonment for life.

[161] Section 6. The offence is committed if a person intentionally penetrates the vagina or anus of another with a part of his body (other than his penis) or anything else. The offence is punishable by a maximum term of imprisonment for life.

[162] Section 7. The offence is committed if a person intentionally touches another and the touching is sexual. The offence is on conviction on indictment punishable by a maximum term of 14 years' imprisonment.

[163] In addition, s 9 makes it an offence for a person aged 18 or over to engage in sexual activity with a child under 16. If the child is aged 13 to 15, the offence is only committed if the perpetrator does not reasonably believe that the child is 16 or over.

6.30 P, by intentionally penetrating D's mouth with his penis, commits the offence of rape of a child under 13. Presumably, D is not an accessory to *that* offence because she can rely on the *Tyrrell* exemption. However, D is guilty of the offence of sexual assault of a child under 13 because she has intentionally touched P and the touching is sexual.[164] Presumably, P is not an accessory to *that* offence because he can rely on the *Tyrrell* principle.

Example 6E

D, a girl aged 12, encourages P, a boy aged 12, to allow D's friend V, a girl aged 12, to perform oral sex on P. P permits V to do this.

6.31 Again, P is guilty of rape of a child under 13. V is not guilty of that offence by virtue of the *Tyrrell* principle.[165] Whether D is guilty of that offence as an accessory depends on whether the *Tyrrell* exemption is available to those who are not victims. In *Tyrrell* the girl was herself the victim of the offence and in all the other cases where the principle has been applied, the person within the protected category has been a victim of the principal offence. On the other hand, there is no case where the courts have expressly held that the exemption is only available to a person who is or would be the victim of the principal offence.

6.32 It seems that Parliament's understanding was that the *Tyrrell* exemption is only available to those who are victims of the principal offence. Section 8 of the Sexual Offences Act 2003 creates an offence of causing or *inciting* a person under 13 to engage in sexual activity:

Example 6F

D, a girl aged 12 encourages P, a boy aged 12, to have sexual intercourse with her.

Example 6G

D, a girl aged 12, encourages P, a boy aged 12, to have sexual intercourse with V, a girl aged 12.

---

[164] To add to the complexity, D and P are also guilty of the offence under section 9 of the Act, namely having sexual activity with a child.

[165] However, like P in example 6D, she is guilty of sexual assault of a child under 13.

6.33   The offence under section 8 is for the protection of children under 13 and in both example 6F and example 6G D falls within that category. In the absence of any express provision to the contrary, the offence under section 8 is subject to the *Tyrrell* exemption. On the other hand, it is significant that in enacting section 8, Parliament did not confine the commission of the offence to persons aged 13 or over. This suggests that Parliament envisaged that there would be circumstances in which a person under 13 could be guilty of the offence. This, in turn, suggests that Parliament assumed that the availability of the *Tyrrell* exemption is dependent on whether D is a victim or potential victim of the principal offence.[166] In other words, Parliament's intention was that, in example 6F, D should be able to avail herself of the *Tyrrell* exemption, but not in example 6G.

The proposals in the CP

6.34   In the CP, the Commission described the *Tyrrell* exemption as being "of uncertain content, and uncertain effect".[167] In setting out its provisional proposals for an inchoate offence of assisting crime, the Commission said provisionally that the exemption should be "stated much more widely than at present".[168] The Commission believed that D ought not to be liable for assisting the commission of a statutory offence if "his conduct is inevitably incidental to its commission and that conduct is not made criminal by that offence".[169]

6.35   The fault element that the Commission was proposing for the offence of assisting crime was "knowledge or belief" on the part of D that P "is doing ... or will do ... acts that do or will involve the commission of an offence by [P]; ...".[170] Some assisters would not only satisfy the "knowledge or belief" test but would also have the more culpable fault element of *intending* that P should commit the offence with their assistance. The Commission inclined to the view that the wider exemption of "incidental involvement" should either not be available in such cases or at least should be available only in a very limited number of cases.[171] It invited comment on what those cases might be.

---

[166] If Parliament had legislated on the basis that the *Tyrrell* exemption applied irrespective of whether D was a victim or prospective victim of the principal offence, it would have stipulated that the offence could only be committed by those aged 13 or over.

[167] Para 2.88. Professor Glanville Williams had previously expressed similar sentiments – "Victims and other exempt parties in crime" (1990) 10 *Legal Studies* 245.

[168] Para 4.102.

[169] Para 4.103.

[170] Para 4.99(1)(a).

[171] Para 4.139

6.36 The fault element that the Commission proposed for encouraging crime was intention on D's part that P should commit the principal offence.[172] It proposed that as a general rule it would be "inappropriate to extend the defence to an encourager".[173] However, it thought that there might be cases, conspicuously those of sexual offences against minors, where the victim "should be exculpated even though she has encouraged rather than assisted in the commission of the offence".[174] The Commission invited comment on what those offences might be.

Responses to the proposals in the CP

6.37 Amongst those respondents who addressed the issue, the majority, with little or no elaboration, agreed with the Commission's proposal for a "more widely" stated exemption. However, Professor Sir John Smith strongly disagreed, describing the Commission's proposal as "dangerously wide":

> If a licensee sells liquor to a constable on duty, I see every reason why the constable should be guilty of [assisting] whether he incited the offence or not. His conduct is inevitably incidental to the commission of the offence, but the offence exists for the protection of the public, not the constable … . The conduct of the recipient of controlled drugs is inevitably incidental to the offence of supplying drugs to another; but if the recipient is buying a ton of the stuff he must surely be guilty of [assisting].

Conclusions

6.38 We now believe that the fact that D's assistance is or will be incidental to the commission of the principal offence should not in itself be a reason for exonerating D. The correct approach is one that is based on statutory interpretation. D should be exempt from liability only if, in enacting the principal offence, it was Parliament's intention to afford protection to a particular category of persons and D falls within that category.

6.39 However, we recognise that, when enacting an offence, Parliament may have more than one objective. We do not think that the exemption should be confined to encouraging or assisting the commission of principal offences the *only* purpose of which is the protection of a particular category of persons. It should suffice that one reason for enacting the offence was to protect a particular category of persons.

6.40 A more difficult issue is whether the exemption should be confined to cases where D would be a "victim" were the principal offence to be committed. Parliament when enacting an offence for the protection of a category of persons does not usually distinguish between different individuals within the category. Instead, each person within the category is considered worthy of protection irrespective of his or her individual traits:

---

[172] Para 4.163(1)(b).

[173] Para 4.167.

[174] Above.

> **Example 6H**
>
> D, a girl aged 15 and sexually very experienced, encourages P, a sexually inexperienced young man aged 18, to engage in sexual activity with her.[175] P knows D is aged 15.

The fact that D is active in tempting P and is sexually very experienced is irrelevant. The offence was enacted for the protection of children under 16 and D is such a person. D is not guilty of inciting P to engage in sexual activity.

6.41 In example 6H, it might be thought that there are two reasons for concluding that D is a "victim". First, if the offence were committed, it would be committed against her. Secondly, she is a "victim" because she is within the protected category and is considered to be in need of protection from others and, despite her sexual experience, from herself:

> **Example 6J**
>
> D, a girl aged 15 and sexually inexperienced, encourages P a young man aged 18, to engage in sexual activity with her friend V, a 15 year old girl, who is sexually very experienced. V also encourages P to engage in sexual activity with her.

V is a "victim" because she is within the protected category and because she is the person against whom the offence would be committed. By contrast, D is a "victim" only because she is a person within the protected category.

6.42 In example 6J, it might be thought that as V's need for protection is no greater than D's, if V is able to rely on the exemption, so too should D. However, by contrast:

> **Example 6K**
>
> D, a precocious and sexually experienced girl aged 14, encourages her brother P, who is aged 18, to engage in sexual activity with D's friend, V, a girl aged 13 and a virgin. V also encourages P to engage in sexual activity with her.

If D is to be exonerated, it can only be because she is a member of the protected category. On balance, we do not believe that it would be right that she should be exempt from liability merely on that basis. D is prepared to encourage or assist the commission of an offence against a vulnerable person. We accept that V will not always be as vulnerable as V is in example 6K. However, we believe that it would be very unsatisfactory for D's liability to depend on the extent of V's vulnerability, not least because the trial process would then involve scrutiny of V's character and previous behaviour.

---

[175] Contrary to the Sexual Offences Act 2003, s 9.

Non-sexual offences

6.43   There is no justification for confining the exemption to sexual offences. Parliament has created offences other than sexual offences for the protection of a particular category of persons. Thus, the Care Standards Act 2000 includes offences designed to protect vulnerable adults residing in care homes. The Asylum and Immigration (Treatment of Claimants, etc) Act 2004 contains offences which are in part designed to protect people who are trafficked for exploitation. The Gangmasters (Licensing) Act 2004 contains offences which are in part designed to protect certain categories of workers.

Recommendation

6.44   **We recommend that it should be a defence to a charge under clause 1 or clause 2 if:**

   (1)   the offence encouraged or assisted is one that exists wholly or in part for the protection of a particular category of persons;

   (2)   D falls within the protected category;

   (3)   D is the person in respect of whom the offence encouraged or assisted was committed or would have been had it had been committed.[176]

DEFENCES THAT WE ARE NOT RECOMMENDING

6.45   In the CP, the Commission identified a number of other potential defences. It concluded that, apart from a defence of withdrawal, none of them were appropriate if D's intention was that P should commit an offence.[177] However, the Commission did consider what defences, if any, should be available to an indifferent assister.

Indifferent assistance in the course of employment

The proposals in the CP

6.46   The Commission provisionally rejected a blanket rule exempting all assistance rendered in the course of employment. It thought that such a rule would, for example, inappropriately exempt from criminal liability the employed bodyguards of a violent professional criminal.[178]

6.47   Instead, the Commission distinguished indictable and summary offences. It provisionally proposed that an employee, D, should not be criminally liable for assisting his or her employer, or a third party, to commit a summary offence provided that the assistance took the form of acts done in the course of D's employment.[179]

---

[176] Clause 6 of the Bill. For explanation, see Appendix A paras A.64 to A.66.

[177] Paras 4.138 and 4.166.

[178] Para 4.107.

[179] Para 4.108.

Responses to the proposal in the CP

6.48 The majority of those who considered the issue agreed that there should be a defence limited to summary offences.

Conclusion

6.49 On balance, we believe that such a defence is neither desirable nor necessary. First, there is no general principle that obeying a superior's unlawful orders is a defence to a crime. We see no justification for creating an exception in the particular case of employees. Secondly, a distinction between indictable and summary offences pays insufficient attention to the fact that some summary offences involve wrongdoing that can lead to very serious consequences and are punishable with imprisonment.[180] Thirdly, we are recommending an offence of acting reasonably in the circumstances. The availability of that defence, irrespective of whether the principal offence is indictable or summary, obviates the need for a defence tailor-made for employees acting in the course of their employment.

Indifferent assistance in the course of a business

6.50 In the CP, the Commission said that there were no legitimate policy reasons for creating a special defence for an indifferent assister whose facilitative act was done in the ordinary course of a business. Indeed the Commission thought that, above all others, business suppliers should be deterred from providing the means by which an offence could be committed.[181] The overwhelming number of respondents who commented on the issue agreed with the Commission.

Conclusion

6.51 We remain convinced that such a defence is not justified. Again, our view is reinforced by the availability of the defence of acting reasonably in the circumstances. The defence would be available to a trader who can prove that he or she acted reasonably in the circumstances.

---

[180] Examples are driving with excess alcohol or while unfit to drive through drink or drugs, contrary to the Road Traffic Act 1988, s 5; assaulting a police officer in the execution of his duty, contrary to the Police Act 1996, s 89 and threatening behaviour with intent to cause fear of immediate unlawful violence, contrary to the Public Order Act 1986, s 4.

[181] Para 4.116.

Withdrawal

6.52 Withdrawal has long been recognised as a defence to secondary liability.[182] The main rationale for the defence is that an accessory who voluntarily changes his or her mind before the principal offence is committed or attempted is significantly less culpable that an accessory who continues to support the commission of the offence.[183] An additional rationale for the defence is that accessories should be provided with an incentive to withdraw.[184]

6.53 By contrast, withdrawal has never been a defence to incitement. Indeed, it might be thought to be anomalous if it were a defence because incitement, being an inchoate offence, crystallises at the moment the encouragement comes to the attention of another person. In principle, any subsequent conduct on the part of D is legally irrelevant.

6.54 However Professor Spencer has suggested that withdrawal should be a defence because if D, prior to the principal offence being committed or attempted, is in a position to try to prevent the commission of the offence, he or she should be encouraged to do so.[185]

The proposals in the CP

6.55 In the CP, the Commission proposed that withdrawal should be a defence to both of the inchoate offences that it was proposing. In the case of assisting crime, it said that the defence should be available only if D took all reasonable steps to prevent the commission of the principal offence.[186] In the case of encouraging, the Commission proposed that the defence should be available if D, with a view to preventing the commission of the principal offence, took all reasonable steps *or* countermanded his or her previous encouragement.[187]

Responses to the proposals in the CP

6.56 The majority of respondents who address the issue thought that there should be a defence of withdrawal. Those who expressed disagreement said that, given the nature of inchoate liability, withdrawal should be relevant only to sentence.

---

[182] *Saunders and Archer* (1576) 2 Plowd 473, 476.

[183] Andrew Ashworth, Commentary on *O'Flaherty* [2004] EWCA Crim 526 [2004] *Criminal Law Review* 751, 752. The fact that the withdrawal is voluntary does not necessarily mean that the motive for withdrawing is honourable.

[184] This rationale assumes that accessories are generally aware that withdrawal is a defence.

[185] *"Trying to help another person commit an offence"* in P Smith (ed) Essays in Honour of JC Smith (1987) 148, 160.

[186] Para 4.135.

[187] Para 4.169.

Conclusion

6.57 We are not persuaded that there should be a defence of withdrawal to the offences that we are recommending. The availability of the defence would be logically indefensible. The arguments that have been advanced in support of the defence focus on D doing something to nullify the effect of his or her previous encouragement or assistance. However, inchoate liability is not dependent on D's conduct having *any* effect on P. D is liable even if his or her conduct has no effect on P and there was never any prospect of P committing the principal offence.

6.58 If it is logically indefensible to extend the defence to inchoate offences, are there other considerations that outweigh the objection founded upon logic? In the CP, the Commission referred to the "the social value of encouraging the reversal of [D's] acts of assistance".[188] However Professor K J M Smith has questioned the Commission's assumption that D will be aware of the defence and would, therefore, be capable of being influenced by its availability.[189] More recently, Profesor Ashworth has observed that "… the language of incentives is only apposite if people … are aware of the legal rule".[190] We believe that providing a providing a defence of withdrawal would have at best a marginal effect in encouraging people to reverse their acts of encouragement or assistance.

Impossibility

The proposals in the CP

6.59 In the CP, the Commission provisionally concluded that the defence should not be available to either of the offences that it was proposing.[191] It thought that D's moral culpability was unaffected by the impossibility, unknown to D, of P committing the principal offence.

Responses to the proposals in the CP

6.60 The overwhelming majority of respondents who commented on the issue thought that impossibility should not be a defence to inchoate offences of encouraging or assisting crime.

Conclusion

6.61 We believe that impossibility should not be a defence to the new offences that we are recommending. D's state of mind and, therefore his or her culpability, is unaffected by the unknown impossibility of the principal offence being committed. Further, if D can be liable notwithstanding that, contrary to D's belief, P never intends to commit the principal offence, it would be illogical if D was able to plead that it would have been impossible to commit the principal offence.

---

[188] Para 4.133.

[189] "The Law Commission Consultation Paper on Complicity: (1) A Blueprint for Rationalism" [1994] *Criminal Law Review* 239, 248.

[190] Commentary on *O'Flaherty* [2004] EWCA Crim 526 in [2004] *Criminal Law Review* 751, 752.

[191] Paras 4.174 to 4.176.

6.62 We do not believe that it is necessary for the Bill to include a clause expressly addressing the issue. In Part 5,[192] we explained that D's liability is in relation to an abstract and not a particular principal offence. In order to be convicted of the new offences, D must do an act that is capable of encouraging or assisting the doing of a criminal act. "Criminal act" refers to no more than the conduct element of the principal offence. If D gives P a weapon, D has done an act capable of assisting the doing of the criminal act of a number of different offences against the person. D's liability will turn on whether he or she intended or expected that P would use the weapon to attack another human being and, if so, with what consequences.

6.63 Accordingly, if D, in return for payment, provides P with a weapon believing that P will use it to attack V1 (intending to kill V1), D is guilty of assisting murder irrespective of whether P uses the weapon to attack anyone. Were P to attack and murder V2, instead of V1, D would be equally guilty of encouraging or assisting murder. If P attacked V2 because V1 was already dead at the time that D provided the weapon, D would still be guilty of encouraging or assisting murder. It may have been impossible for V1 to be murdered but, nonetheless, D had done an act capable of encouraging or assisting the conduct element of murder, namely an attack on any human being.

[192] Para 5.13 above.

PART 7
INFINITE INCHOATE LIABILITY AND RELATED ISSUES

INTRODUCTION

7.1 In this Part, we consider a particular aspect of an issue which, while not unique to inchoate offences, has a heightened significance in the context of inchoate liability. The issue is the over-extension of criminal liability. Hitherto, we have described our scheme of inchoate liability by reference to the paradigm case: *D encouraging or assisting P to commit an offence* ("the principal offence"). In the paradigm case, D's conduct is only one step removed from the principal offence. However, that will not always be the case:

Example 7A

D, knowing that P is planning to act as X's getaway driver in a robbery, lends a car to P so that P can provide the assistance to X.

Example 7B

D, knowing that P intends to distribute a leaflet encouraging X to commit a racially motivated assault, provides P with the means of producing the leaflets.

Example 7C

D encourages P to encourage X to rape V.

At common law, if X commits the robbery, the assault and the rape respectively, both D and P will be accessories to and guilty of the principal offence. The doctrine of secondary liability does not exonerate D merely because his or her conduct was more than one step removed from the commission of the principal offence.

7.2   However, in each of the three examples, X may not commit the principal offence. If so, at common law the issue of D's liability only arises in example 7C. In examples 7A and 7B, D would not be liable because D's contribution consists of assistance and at common law there is no inchoate liability for assisting the commission of an offence.[1] By contrast, in example 7C, D's contribution consists of encouragement. D would be criminally liable because the common law recognises not only an offence of incitement but also an offence of incitement to incite.[2] D is guilty of inciting P to incite rape. As with secondary liability, D is not exonerated merely because his or her encouragement is more than one step removed from the principal offence.

7.3   The approach of the common law in recognising an offence of incitement to incite is defensible. The inchoate offences of attempt, conspiracy and incitement punish conduct not because it is harmful in itself but because, by seeking to encourage or assist the commission of an offence, it enhances the prospects of harmful consequences occurring. They are offences which necessarily involve conduct that is one step removed from the commission of the principal offence. Logically, there is no reason why inchoate liability should not attach to conduct that is two steps removed. If D can be liable for encouraging P to commit an offence, why should D not be liable for encouraging P to encourage X to commit an offence? Further, if D can be liable for conduct that is two steps removed, why should D not be liable for conduct that is three or more steps removed? In logic and in principle, there is no impediment to an endless chain and almost infinite inchoate liability.

7.4   Likewise, in logic and in principle, it ought to be permissible to base criminal liability on a combination of *different* inchoate offences:

Example 7D

D1 and D2 are rival drug dealers who are increasingly concerned about the activities of another rival, V. They wish to eliminate V but are anxious to distance themselves from the murder. They agree that they will encourage P, who they know has his or her own reasons for eliminating V, to murder V. They meet with P and encourage P to murder V.

If P murders V, D1 and D2 will be accessories to and guilty of murder. Should P not even attempt to murder V, D1 and D2 are nevertheless guilty of conspiracy to incite murder.[3]

---

[1]   However, under the scheme that we are recommending, the issue of D's liability in examples 7A and 7B would arise.

[2]   *Sirat* (1985) 83 Cr App R 41.

[3]   Criminal Law Act 1977, s 1(1) which preserved the common law.

7.5   However, there is a strong argument against both infinite inchoate liability and liability based on combining different inchoate offences. It is that such liability represents an unlimited and unwarranted extension of the criminal law. It allows D, because of potentially harmful consequences that may flow if P does commit the principal offence, to be criminally liable on the basis of conduct that is very remote from the prospective principal offence and consequent harm. On this view, the further removed and, therefore, the more remote D's conduct is from the prospective principal offence, the more cautious the law should be before imposing criminal liability. Further, encouraging or assisting the commission of an offence is by its very nature more remote from the prospective principal offence than simply conspiring or attempting to commit it. This is because whether or not the principal offence is ultimately committed depends on the actions of the person encouraged or assisted. In contrast, in cases of conspiracy and attempt, it is the actions of the conspirators and the person trying to commit the principal offence which determine whether the prospective principal offence is committed.

THE CURRENT LAW

7.6   The current law, a mixture of common law and sporadic statutory provisions, is an incoherent and confusing muddle:

   (1)   it is not an offence for D to *assist* P to assist or encourage X to murder V or for D to incite P to *assist* X to murder V[4] but it is an offence for D to incite P to incite X to murder V;[5]

   (2)   it is not an offence for D to incite X and P to conspire to murder V.[6] It is, however an offence for D and P to conspire to incite X to murder V;[7]

   (3)   it is an offence for D to incite P to attempt to murder V and for D to attempt to incite P to murder V.[8] However, it is not an offence for D to attempt to conspire with P to murder V;[9]

   (4)   it is not an offence for D to attempt to commit an offence as an accessory.[10] It is unclear whether it is an offence for D to incite P to commit an offence as an accessory.[11]

---

[4]   Unless, in each case, X murders or attempts to murder V in which case D and P are accessories to and guilty of murder or attempted murder.

[5]   *Sirat* (1985) 83 Cr App R 41.

[6]   Criminal Law Act 1977, s 5(7).

[7]   Criminal Law Act, s 1(1). In its Report on Conspiracy and Criminal Law Reform (1976) Law Com No 76, the Commission had expressly said (para 1.44) that an offence of conspiracy to incite was justified.

[8]   *Banks and Banks* (1873) 12 Cox CC 393; *Ransford* (1874) 13 Cox CC 9, 16 to 17.

[9]   Criminal Attempts Act 1981, s 1(4)(a). Again, it is right to say that in Inchoate Offences: Conspiracy, Attempt and Incitement (1973) Law Commission Working Paper No 50, the Commission expressed (para 44) the provisional view that an offence of attempt to commit conspiracy could not be justified. The Commission confirmed its view in Attempt, and Impossibility in relation to Attempt, Conspiracy and Incitement (1980) Law Com No 102 para 2.122.

THE PROPOSALS IN THE CP

7.7 In the CP, the Commission's provisional conclusion was that each of the two new inchoate offences that it was proposing, encouraging crime and assisting crime, should not be able to be committed in respect of any inchoate offence, including the new offences themselves.[12] Its reason was that D's conduct would be "too remote from the commission of the principal crime for it to be justified to pursue him".[13] The Commission drew no distinction between encouraging crime and assisting crime despite the fact that the fault element it was proposing for the former was narrower than that for the latter.

7.8 Conversely, the Commission thought that, if the law of secondary liability was put on an inchoate basis, there was no obvious reason of policy to prevent D being liable for conspiring to encourage crime or conspiring to assist crime and for attempting to encourage crime or attempting to assist crime.[14]

Responses to the proposals in the CP

7.9 The overwhelming majority of respondents who considered the issue agreed with the Commission that it should not be possible to encourage or assist any inchoate offence. Respondents were concerned that criminal liability should not be extended too far and that there had to be limits to the scope of inchoate liability. A smaller but significant majority agreed that there should be liability for conspiring and attempting to encourage or assist the commission of an offence.

CONCLUSIONS

Committing the clause 1 offence or a clause 2 offence by encouraging or assisting another person to commit those offences

7.10 It has to be borne in mind that D satisfies the conduct element of both the clause 1 offence and the clause 2 offence by merely doing an act that is capable of encouraging or assisting. Further, even in cases where D's encouragement or assistance is only two steps removed from the prospective principal offence, P may never act upon D's encouragement or assistance and, in turn, X may never act upon P's encouragement or assistance. We think that these are important considerations for the purposes of determining the circumstances in which D should incur liability for encouraging or assisting P to encourage or assist X to commit an offence.

---

[10] Criminal Attempts Act 1981, s 1(4)(d). An example would be D attempting, but failing, to hire a getaway car for use in a robbery that P goes on to commit without any assistance from D. The Commission in Attempt, and Impossibility in relation to Attempt, Conspiracy and Incitement (1976) Law Com No 76 recommended (para 2.123) that an attempt to aid, abet, counsel or procure the commission of an offence should not be an offence.

[11] See Part 3 paras 3.39 to 3.43 above.

[12] Para 4.184.

[13] Para 4.183.

[14] Para 4.186.

7.11 Our recommendations build on the common law in relation to incitement. The common law recognises an offence of incitement to incite.[15] In our view, it is right to do so. Although it is not entirely free from doubt, the preferred view is that in order to be guilty of incitement, D must intend that the principal offence is committed (or, at least, that P should be encouraged to commit it).[16] Accordingly, D can only be guilty of inciting P to incite X to murder V if it was D's intention that P should incite X (or that P should be encouraged to incite X). We believe that is a sufficiently stringent requirement to justify D incurring criminal liability for conduct that is more than one step removed from the principal offence.

7.12 The new offences that we are recommending, like those proposed by the Commission in the CP, have different fault elements. The clause 1 offence requires that D must intend to encourage or assist the doing of a criminal act. In line with the common law of incitement, we believe that in cases where D encourages or assists P *intending* that P should encourage or assist X to commit an offence, D ought to be liable. The fact that D's act is a step further removed from the principal offence should not, given D's highly culpable state of mind, be a bar to liability in such cases. Further, given D's culpable state of mind, D ought to be liable irrespective of how many steps his or her conduct is removed from the principal offence.

7.13 On the other hand, the clause 2(1) and 2(2) offences only require D to *believe* that P will commit a criminal act and that D's act will encourage or assist P to commit a criminal act. In the light of the considerations to which we have just referred, we believe that it would be an over-extension of criminal liability if D were to be criminally liable for the clause 2 offences in cases where he or she has encouraged or assisted P to encourage or assist X.

7.14 In cases where D does encourage or assist P intending that P should encourage or assist X, P may or may not intend that X should commit the principal offence:

Example 7E

D encourages P to hire X to murder V who has been having an affair with P's wife.

Example 7F

P tells D that, in return for a substantial payment, he is contemplating selling a firearm to X although he believes that X intends to use it to kill V. D, who hates V, urges P to provide the firearm to X.

In example 7E, if P were to encourage X, he would do so with the intention that X should murder V. By contrast, in example 7F, were P to sell the firearm to X, he would do so for the purpose of making a profit but without intending that X should murder V.

[15] *Sirat* (1985) 83 Cr App R 41.

[16] See para 3.45 above.

7.15 We believe that in each example D ought to be liable. It is D's state of mind that is critical. If it is D's intention that P should encourage or assist X, his or her conduct should not be considered too remote from the principal offence merely because, were P to encourage or assist X, P would not intend X to commit the principal offence.

Recommendation

7.16 **We recommend that D may commit the clause 1 offence but not a clause 2 offence by:**

> **(1)   doing an act capable of encouraging or assisting P to do an act capable of encouraging or assisting X to do a criminal act , and**

> **(2)   intending that P should do, or be encouraged to do, the act.[17]**

7.17 If D encourages or assists P to encourage or assist X to commit an offence, D is encouraging or assisting P to do an act which, were P to do it and were X to commit the offence, would render P an accessory to the offence. In Part 3,[18] we referred to the uncertainty that exists at common law as to whether D can be convicted in such circumstances of not merely incitement to incite but of incitement to commit the principal offence:

> **Example 7G**
>
> D encourages P to encourage X to rape V. X ignores P's encouragement.

Although D is guilty of incitement to incite rape, according to *Bodin*[19], D is not guilty of inciting rape because had X raped V, P would have been guilty of the offence but as an accessory and not as a principal offender.

7.18 Simester and Sullivan have criticised *Bodin*[20] and we recognise the force of the criticism. The effect of *Bodin* was to prevent D incurring liability for incitement if D encouraged P to *assist* X to commit an offence but X did not commit or attempt to commit the offence.[21] By contrast, however, under our recommendations it will be possible to convict D of the clause 1 offence if he or she encourages or assists P to commit the clause 1 offence or a clause 2 offence. There is no longer the gap which existed at common law.[22]

---

[17] Clause 2(5)(a) of the Bill gives effect to our recommendation by providing that D cannot commit a clause 2 offence by doing an act capable of encouraging X to do an act capable of encouraging or assisting P to commit an offence.

[18] Paras 3.39 to 3.43.

[19] [1979] *Criminal Law Review* 176.

[20] Para 3.43 above

[21] There was no problem if D encouraged P to encourage X. D was guilty of incitement to incite - Sirat (1985) 83 Cr App R 41.

[22] We acknowledge that there is a gap if D encourages or assists P to *procure* X to commit an offence which X does not commit. We will be addressing this issue in our report on secondary liability.

Committing the clause 1 offence or a clause 2 offence by encouraging or assisting others to conspire to commit an offence

7.19   Parliament's decision in 1977 to abolish the offence of incitement to commit conspiracy[23] was not based on any Law Commission recommendation.[24] In abolishing the offence, Parliament may have thought that at common law there was no offence of incitement to incite an offence. In 1983, the Court of Appeal confirmed that there was such an offence.[25] This led the Law Commission in 1989 to say that the law had "reached the point of absurdity":

> If the evidence shows that D incited [X] to agree with [P] to wound G, section 5(7) of the Criminal Law Act 1977 apparently prevents a charge against D of incitement to conspire or of incitement to incite. But if D incites [P] to incite [X] … to wound G, D can be charged with incitement to incite. Such an absurd distinction cannot be restated in a code. [26]

The Commission recommended that conspiracy should cease to be excluded from the scope of incitement.[27]

7.20   Again, we believe that D should only be liable for encouraging or assisting X and P to conspire to commit an offence if D intends that X and P should form the conspiracy or that X and P should be encouraged to do so:

Example 7H

D knows that X and P, normally rival drug dealers, are concerned about the activities of V another drug dealer. D, who hates V, makes a room available to X and P so that they can hatch a plot to murder V. The meeting breaks up in acrimony without any agreement having been reached.

Under our recommendations, D has committed the clause 1 offence because D has done an act capable of encouraging or assisting X and P to conspire to murder intending that they should commit the offence of conspiracy to murder. However, D would not commit the clause 2(1) offence if, purely for financial gain, D hired the room to X and P believing that D and P wanted the room in order to negotiate an agreement to murder V.

Recommendation

7.21   **We recommend that D may commit the clause 1 offence but not a clause 2 offence by:**

[23]   Criminal Law Act 1977, s 5(7).

[24]   It is true that in Inchoate Offences: Conspiracy, Attempt and Incitement (1973) Law Commission Working Paper No 50, the Commission expressed (para 44) the provisional view that an offence of incitement to commit conspiracy could not be justified. However, in its Report on Conspiracy and Criminal Law Reform (1976) Law Com No 76, the Commission made no recommendation.

[25]   *Sirat* (1985) 83 Cr App R 41.

[26]   Criminal Law: A Criminal Code for England and Wales, vol 2 Commentary on Draft Criminal Code Bill (1989) Law Com No 177, para 13.13.

[27]   Para 13.15.

(1)   **doing an act capable of encouraging or assisting X and P to conspire to commit an offence; and**

(2)   **intending that X and P should conspire, or be encouraged to conspire, to commit the offence.**[28]

Committing the clause 1 offence or a clause 2 offence by encouraging or assisting another person to attempt to commit an offence

7.22   At common law a charge of incitement to commit attempt is very uncommon because D will nearly always be encouraging P to commit the full offence. However, we provided an example in Part 3.[29] Although Parliament abolished the offence of incitement to commit conspiracy, it left untouched the offence of incitement to commit attempt.

7.23   The need for consistency of approach requires that D should be liable for doing an act capable of encouraging or assisting P to attempt to commit an offence only if it was his or her intention that P should attempt to commit the offence. In practise, we find it difficult to envisage a case where D would not have that intention.

Recommendation

7.24   **We recommend that D may commit the clause 1 offence but not a clause 2 offence by:**

(1)   **doing an act capable of encouraging or assisting P to attempt to commit an offence; and**

(2)   **intending that P should attempt, or be encouraged to attempt, to commit the offence.**[30]

---

[28]   Para 10 of sch 1 Part 1 and para 18 of sch 1 Part 2 to the Bill give effect to our recommendation by providing that D cannot commit the clause 2 offences by doing an act capable of encouraging or assisting conspiracy, whether a statutory conspiracy or a common law conspiracy.

[29]   Example 3H at para 3.38.

[30]   Para 11 of sch 1 Part 1 and para 19(1) of sch 1 Part 2 to the Bill give effect to our recommendation by providing that D cannot commit a clause 2 offence by doing an act capable of encouraging or assisting P to attempt to commit an offence.

PART 8
EXTRA-TERRITORIAL JURISDICTION

INTRODUCTION

8.1 The common law of England and Wales evolved over centuries when relatively few offences were committed across national frontiers. However, the last fifty years has witnessed the phenomenon of globalisation. Criminal organisations have not been slow to exploit the opportunities afforded by the emergence of that phenomenon. Thus, although most serious crimes are still local in their commission and effect, a small but significant number cross national boundaries. This development is particularly pertinent to inchoate offences. Thus, it is not uncommon to encounter conspiracies formed in one country to import drugs, firearms, people or rare animals into another country. Similarly, there are multifarious ways in which encouragement or assistance may be sent from and to any place in the world.

GENERAL PRINCIPLES

8.2 The primary basis of English criminal jurisdiction is territorial. A court in England and Wales has jurisdiction to try a person, whether or not a British citizen, for an offence committed in England and Wales.[31] However, apart from statutory exceptions,[32] a person cannot be tried within the jurisdiction for an offence committed outside the jurisdiction. In addition, when construing a statute creating an offence, there is a strong presumption that Parliament did not intend that conduct occurring outside the jurisdiction should be an offence triable within the jurisdiction.[33]

8.3 In some cases, it may not be obvious whether or not an offence has been committed within the jurisdiction. Prior to 1970, the orthodox view was that, for the purposes of determining jurisdiction, the last element needed to complete the offence had to take place within the jurisdiction.[34] It followed that if an offence consisted of both a conduct element and a consequence element, the consequence had to take effect within the jurisdiction.

---

[31] In order to avoid wearisome repetition, instead of referring to "England and Wales" we will sometimes refer just to "the jurisdiction".

[32] Statutory exceptions include the Offences against the Person Act 1861, s 9 (commission of murder or manslaughter by a British subject on land overseas); the Anti-Terrorism, Crime and Security Act 2001, s 109 (bribery and corruption committed outside the United Kingdom); the Sexual Offences Act 2003, s 72 (commission of certain sexual offences outside the United Kingdom by British citizens or residents of the United Kingdom); Criminal Law Act 1977, s 1A (conspiracy to commit a crime abroad).

[33] *Treacy* [1971] AC 537, 551 by Lord Reid; *Air India v Wiggins* [1980] 1 WLR 815.

[34] *Ellis* [1899] 1 QB 230; *Harden* [1963] 1 QB 8. Professor Glanville Williams, "Venue and the Ambit of Criminal Law" (1965) 81 *Law Quarterly Review*, 276, 518 described this as the "terminatory theory of jurisdiction". -

8.4 However, in 1970, Lord Diplock challenged the orthodox view.[35] He concluded that, provided a statutory offence contains no express geographical limitation, comity only precludes a person being tried for the offence within the jurisdiction if neither the conduct nor the consequences take place within the jurisdiction:

> ... each sovereign state should refrain from punishing persons for their conduct within the territory of another sovereign state where that conduct has had no harmful consequences within the territory of the state which imposes the punishment. ... . In my view, where the definition of [an] offence contains a requirement that the described conduct of the accused should be followed by described consequences the implied exclusion is limited to cases where *neither* the conduct *nor* its harmful consequences took place in England and Wales.[36]

8.5 However, cases of conspiracy apart, the English courts continued to apply the terminatory theory of jurisdiction[37] until *Smith (Wallace Duncan) (No 1)*.[38] In that case, the Court of Appeal held that the courts of England and Wales had jurisdiction to try a charge of obtaining by deception where the last act, the obtaining, took place in the city of New York. Subsequently, however, in *Manning*,[39] a differently constituted Court of Appeal refused to follow *Smith (Wallace Duncan) (No 1)*.

8.6 More recently, in *Smith (Wallace Duncan) (No 4)*[40] the Court of Appeal has held that where a substantial measure of the activities constituting an offence takes place within the jurisdiction, the courts of England and Wales have jurisdiction to try the offence, irrespective of where the last element of the offence occurred. The policy that underpins the decision is that, given the prevalence of international financial activity, jurisdiction should not be restricted by the technicality of the terminatory theory.

INCHOATE OFFENCES

8.7 Inchoate offences present particular difficulties because frequently all of the activities that constitute an inchoate offence take place outside the jurisdiction of the territory where it is intended that the principal offence should be committed. Thus, D and P agree in New York to commit a robbery in London. Alternatively, D in Paris sends a letter to P in Rome urging P to murder V in London.

---

[35] *Treacy* [1971] AC 537, 561 to 564.

[36] Above, 564 (emphasis in original).

[37] *Tirado* (1974) 59 Cr App R 80; *Beck* [1985] 1 WLR 22; *Thompson* [1984] 1 WLR 962; *Nanayakkara* [1987] 1 WLR 265.

[38] [1996] 2 Cr App R 1.

[39] [1999] QB 980.

[40] [2004] 3 WLR 229.

Conspiracy

Introduction

8.8   The offence of conspiracy is complete as soon as an agreement to commit an offence is formed:

Example 8A

P1 and P2 agree in Calais to commit a robbery in Dover.

If the general principles that apply to substantive offences were applied, P1 and P2 could not be tried within the jurisdiction for conspiracy to rob because the offence has been committed in France. However, the courts have displayed a readiness to depart from the general principles.

Conspiracy formed out of the jurisdiction to commit a crime within the jurisdiction

8.9   In *DPP v Doot*[41] the House of Lords held that a conspiracy formed abroad to commit an offence in England and Wales was triable within the jurisdiction provided an "overt act" in pursuance of the conspiracy had taken place within the jurisdiction. In *Somchai Liangsinpraseret v United States*[42] the Privy Council dispensed with the need for any "overt act" within the jurisdiction.[43] Having noted that inchoate offences were developed with the principal objective of frustrating the commission of a contemplated crime by enabling the authorities to arrest offenders before the commission of the crime, Lord Griffiths observed:

> If the inchoate crime is aimed at England with the consequent injury to English society, why should the English courts not accept jurisdiction to try it if the authorities can lay hands on the offenders, either because they come within the jurisdiction or through extradition procedures? … . Crime is now established on an international scale and the common law must face this new reality. Their Lordships can find nothing in precedent, comity or good sense that should inhibit the common law from regarding as justiciable in England inchoate crimes committed abroad which are intended to result in the commission of offences in England.[44]

---

[41]   [1973] AC 807.

[42]   [1991] 1 AC 225.

[43]   This is true of both common law and statutory conspiracies – *Sansom* [1991] 2 QB 130.

[44]   [1991] AC 225, 251.

Conspiracy formed within the jurisdiction to commit a crime abroad

8.10 By contrast, the common law has adopted a restrictive approach to conspiracies formed within the jurisdiction to commit a crime abroad. In *Board of Trade v Owen*[45] it was held that a conspiracy formed within England and Wales to commit an offence abroad is not triable within the jurisdiction.[46]

STATUTE

8.11 However, Parliament has subsequently enacted that parties who conspire within the jurisdiction to commit an offence in a country outside the United Kingdom may be indicted and tried within the jurisdiction if the act:

(1) would be a criminal offence in the foreign country concerned;

(2) would be an offence under English law if committed within the jurisdiction; and

(3) a party to the agreement:

(a) did anything within the jurisdiction in relation to the agreement before its formation; or

(b) became a party to the agreement within the jurisdiction; or

(c) did or omitted anything within the jurisdiction in pursuance of the agreement.[47]

Incitement

8.12 The offence of incitement is complete as soon as the incitement comes to the attention of the intended recipient:

Example 8B

D in New York phones P in Chicago and encourages P to commit a robbery in London.

The offence is committed outside the jurisdiction and, again, were the general principles that apply to substantive offences to be applied, D cannot be tried within the jurisdiction for incitement to commit robbery.

---

[45] [1957] AC 602.

[46] Unless the principal offence is one of those offences that can be tried in England and Wales even if committed abroad, eg murder or manslaughter committed by a British citizen in a country outside the United Kingdom – Offences against the Person Act 1861, s 9.

[47] Criminal Law Act 1977, s 1A (inserted by the Criminal Justice (Terrorism and Conspiracy) Act 1998, s 5(1)).

An act of incitement done abroad to commit an offence within the jurisdiction

8.13 Although there is no authority which confirms that the principles that apply to conspiracy also apply to incitement, there is nothing to suggest that in *Liangsiriprasert v United States* Lord Griffiths intended his observations to be confined to conspiracy. Accordingly, in example 8B, a court in England and Wales would have jurisdiction to try D for incitement to commit robbery.[48]

An act of incitement done within the jurisdiction to commit an offence abroad

COMMON LAW

8.14 By analogy with conspiracy, the general rule is that if D in England incites P to commit an offence abroad, at common law the incitement is not triable within the jurisdiction. However, as with conspiracy, the incitement will be triable if the principal offence is one that, although committed abroad, can be tried within the jurisdiction.[49]

STATUTE

8.15 In contrast to conspiracy, Parliament has not enacted a general provision enabling incitements to commit offences abroad to be tried within the jurisdiction. Instead, there are specific statutory provisions which make it an offence triable in England and Wales to incite the commission abroad of certain types of offences.[50]

---

[48] In *DPP v Stonehouse* [1978] AC 255 D faked his death in Miami so that his wife in England, who was not a party to the fraud, could claim on life insurance policies. The House of Lords held that a court in England and Wales had jurisdiction to try D for *attempting* to obtain property by deception even though no act constituting the attempt had taken place in England or Wales.

[49] Again, there is no authority.

[50] Eg, Sexual Offences (Conspiracy and Incitement) Act 1996, s 2 which makes it an offence to incite certain sexual offences against children outside the United Kingdom; Terrorism Act 2000, s 59 which makes it an offence to incite act of terrorism wholly or partly outside the United Kingdom; Criminal Justice Act 1993, s 5(4) (inciting offences of fraud and dishonesty).

OUR RECOMMENDATIONS IN RELATION TO THE NEW OFFENCES

8.16   In this report, our objective is to set out a comprehensive statutory scheme of inchoate liability for encouraging or assisting crime to replace the common law rules. A comprehensive statutory scheme cannot disregard the issue of extra-territorial jurisdiction. We have explained that, while the courts have considered the issue in relation to conspiracy and to a lesser extent attempt, there is a dearth of authority in relation to incitement. In this section, we will set out our recommendations in relation to the new offences. However, we emphasise that, were our recommendations to be implemented, only the common law offence of incitement would be abolished. Our recommendations do not impact on statutory offences of incitement.[51] Accordingly, statutory offences of incitement that have their own jurisdictional rules will continue to be governed by those rules.

Principal offence anticipated to take place wholly or partly in England and Wales

8.17   We agree with Lord Griffiths that it should be an offence triable in England Wales to commit an inchoate offence abroad intending that it should lead to the commission of a principal offence within the jurisdiction. However, we would go further:

Example 8C

D sends an e-mail from Los Angeles to P in New York. D urges P to fly to Europe to murder V. D says that V may or may not be in London but that, if V is not in London, he will be in his summer villa in France. Acting on intelligence, the police arrest P before P can murder V.

Arguably, because D cannot be sure that V will be in London, D does not *intend* the principal offence to be committed within the jurisdiction. However, D believes that the principal offence might be committed within the jurisdiction and that should be sufficient to ground liability.

8.18   **We recommend that D should be guilty of one of the new offences if D knew or believed that the principal offence might be committed wholly or partly in England and Wales, irrespective of where D did the act capable of encouraging or assisting the commission of the principal offence.[52]**

---

[51]   Apart from sch 1 Part 1 of the Bill which provides that D cannot be convicted a cl 2 offence for encouraging or assisting P to incite X to commit certain statutory offences of incitement, eg Offences against the Person Act 1861, s 4 (soliciting to murder).

[52]   Clause 7(1) of the Bill. For explanation, see Appendix A paras A.69 to A.70.

Principal offence not anticipated to take place wholly or partly in England and Wales

D's act done within the jurisdiction

8.19   We explained above that, by analogy with conspiracy, at common law an act of incitement done within the jurisdiction to commit a principal offence abroad is not triable in England and Wales. In relation to conspiracy, the common law position was radically altered by section 1A of the Criminal Law Act 1977.[53] The section requires that the conduct that is the subject of the conspiracy must be an offence under the law of England and Wales and also under the law of the foreign territory. It is the double requirement of criminality, together with the requirement that there has to be some act of D within the jurisdiction, which justifies the conspiracy being triable within the jurisdiction.

8.20   Simester and Sullivan describe the breadth of coverage of section 1A as "enormous", citing an example of two foreign tourists in London agreeing to cheat on the Paris Metro.[54] However, as a safeguard, the Attorney General must give consent to any prosecution. Further, the section enables prosecutions to be brought in England and Wales thereby avoiding the need for possibly protracted proceedings under the Extradition Act 2003.[55]

8.21   Accordingly, we believe that for the new offences that we are recommending, there should be a similar provision to section 1A which would inculpate D in the following example:

> **Example 8D**
>
> D in London sends an e-mail to P in Newcastle encouraging P to commit theft in Madrid. Theft is an offence in Spain.

8.22   **We recommend that D may commit one of the new offences if :**

   (1)   D does an act wholly or partly within the jurisdiction capable of encouraging or assisting a person to commit what would be a principal offence under the law of England and Wales;

   (2)   D knows or believes that the principal offence might be committed wholly or partly in a place outside the jurisdiction;

   (3)   the principal offence is also an offence under the law of the territory where D knows or believes that it might wholly or partly take place.[56]

---

[53]   As inserted by Criminal Justice (Terrorism and Conspiracy) Act 1993. See para 8.11.

[54]   *Criminal Law Theory and Doctrine* (2nd ed 2003) p 321.

[55]   In addition, the witnesses to the inchoate offence are likely to be resident in England and Wales.

[56]   Schedule 2 para 2(1) to the Bill. For explanation, see Appendix A paras A75 to 76.

8.23 However, subject to one exception, we do not believe that D should be liable for one of the new offences if the principal offence is *not* an offence under the law of the foreign territory. The exception is if the principal offence would be triable within England and Wales were it to be committed in the foreign territory:

Example 8E

D sends an e-mail from London to P, a British citizen, in country x. D urges P to murder V, a British citizen who is visiting country x. Under the law of country x, it is not an offence for a British citizen to kill another British citizen.

If P did murder V, P could be tried in England and Wales despite the fact that the murder of V is not an offence under the law of country x.[57] If P could be tried within the jurisdiction for the principal offence, it also ought to be possible to try D within the jurisdiction for encouraging or assisting its commission.

8.24 **We recommend that D may commit one of the new offences if:**

   (1)   D does an act wholly or partly within the jurisdiction capable of encouraging or assisting a person to commit a principal offence under the law of England and Wales;

   (2)   D knows or believes that the principal offence might be committed wholly or partly in a place outside the jurisdiction;

   (3)   the principal offence, if committed in that place, is an offence for which the perpetrator could be tried in England and Wales (if he or she satisfies a relevant citizenship, nationality or residence condition, if any).[58]

D's act takes place wholly outside the jurisdiction

8.25 Subject to one exception, D should not be guilty of one of the new offences if the principal offence is not anticipated to take place within the jurisdiction and D's act of encouragement or assistance takes place wholly outside the jurisdiction. The exception is if D, were he or she to commit the principal offence in the foreign territory, could be tried in England and Wales for the offence:

Example 8F

D, a British citizen, is on holiday with P and V, both British citizens, in France. Following a heated argument, D encourages P to murder V in France.

Example 8G

D, an *American* citizen, is on holiday with P and V, both British citizens, in France. Following a heated argument, D encourages P to murder V in France.

---

[57]   Offences against the Person Act 1861, s 9.

[58]   Para 1(1) of sch 2 to the Bill. For explanation, see Appendix A paras A73 to A74.

In example 8F, D could be tried in England and Wales were he or she to murder V in France because D is a British citizen. By contrast, in example 8G, D could not be tried in England and Wales were he or she to murder V in France because D is an American citizen.

8.26 **We recommend that D may commit one of the new offences if:**

  (1) D's conduct takes place wholly outside the jurisdiction;

  (2) D knows or believes that the principal offence might be committed wholly or partly in a place outside the jurisdiction;

  (3) D could be tried in England and Wales if he or she committed the principal act in that place.[59]

Role of the Attorney General

8.27 Section 1A of the Criminal Law Act 1977 provides that proceedings in respect of a conspiracy to commit an offence outside the jurisdiction can only be instituted with the consent of the Attorney General. The requirement is a sensible safeguard to ensure that proceedings are only brought in appropriate cases. We believe that there should be a similar requirement in relation to the new offences.

8.28 **We recommend that, in cases where it cannot be proved that D knew or believed that the principal offence might take place wholly or partly within the jurisdiction, no proceedings may be instituted except by or with the consent of the Attorney General.[60]**

IMPLICATIONS FOR CONSPIRACY

8.29 We think that it is desirable that there should be a correspondence between the jurisdictional rules governing inchoate offences of encouraging or assisting crime and the jurisdictional rules for conspiracy. Accordingly, we suggest that consideration be given to providing a statutory scheme of jurisdictional rules for conspiracy to run in tandem with the scheme that we are recommending for the new offences that we are recommending.

POSTSCRIPT

European arrest warrant

Introduction

8.30 Having described the extra-territorial provisions that we are recommending, we believe it might be helpful to provide a brief outline of the European arrest warrant.

---

[59] Schedule 2 para 3 to the Bill. For explanation, see Appendix A paras A77 to A 78.

[60] Clause 8 of the Bill.

8.31   In 2003 Parliament enacted the Extradition Act in order to discharge the United Kingdom's duty to transpose into national law the obligations imposed on it by the European Council Framework Decision of 13 June 2002 on the European arrest warrant and the surrender procedures between member states ("the Framework Decision").

8.32   The European arrest warrant represents the response of member states of the European Union to the problem of those who, facing prosecution or imprisonment in one member state, seek refuge in another member state in the hope of evading trial or imprisonment. Member states recognised that previous procedures founded on bilateral treaties had not always worked effectively. Instead, member states agreed to implement a simplified system of surrender of suspected or sentenced persons.

8.33   The chosen mechanism was a European arrest warrant based on a principle of mutual recognition. The warrant is a judicial decision issued by one member state ("the issuing state") for the arrest and surrender by another member state ("the executing state") of the person named in the warrant ("the requested person"). The surrender is so that the issuing state can conduct a criminal prosecution or execute a custodial sentence in respect of the offence specified in the warrant ("the extradition offence").

8.34   The warrant may only be issued in respect of an offence punishable by the law of the issuing state by a sentence of at least 12 months or, where a sentence has been passed on the requested person, by a sentence of at least four months.

8.35   The Framework Decision lists kinds of criminal conduct, described in general terms, which it is assumed will feature in the criminal law of member states, for example murder, armed robbery and trafficking in human beings ("the framework list offences"). A warrant that specifies such an offence permits the executing state to surrender the requested person to the issuing state irrespective of whether the offence is a criminal offence under the law of the executing state.[61] In other words, if the offence is a framework list offence, there is an assumption of double criminality.

8.36   The operation of the European arrest is not confined to framework offences. However, if the offence is not a framework list offence, the Framework Decision entitles the executing state to refuse to accede to the request for surrender if the conduct referred to in the warrant does not constitute an offence under its own law.

8.37   The Framework Decision also enables the legislature of each member state to pass legislation preventing its courts from executing a European arrest warrant if the warrant relates to an offence which:

(1)   is regarded by the law of the executing state as having been committed in whole or in part in its own territory; or

---

[61]   However, under the law of the issuing state, the offence must be punishable by a term of imprisonment of at least three years.

(2)   was committed outside the territory of the issuing state and the law of the executing state does not allow prosecution for the offence when committed outside its own territory.

The Extradition Act 2003

8.38   In order to give effect to the Framework Decision, Parliament enacted the Extradition Act 2003. The Act defines the offences in respect of which the issuing state may seek the surrender of the requested person. Importantly, it sets out the territorial conditions that have to be satisfied in respect of an offence ("the extradition offence") before the courts of England and Wales may order the extradition of the requested person to the issuing state.[62]

THE TERRITORIAL CONDITIONS

The offence is committed outside the territory of the issuing state

8.39   Where the conduct that constitutes the extradition offence occurred outside the territory of the issuing state, the territorial conditions that must be satisfied before a court in England and Wales may order extradition of the requested person to the issuing state are:

(1)   the equivalent conduct would constitute an extra-territorial offence under the law of England and Wales punishable with imprisonment for a term of 12 months or more;[63] or

(2)   no part of the conduct occurred in the United Kingdom and the conduct would constitute an offence under the law of England and Wales punishable with imprisonment for a term of 12 months or more; or

(3)   no part of the conduct occurred in the United Kingdom and the conduct constitutes or, if committed within the United Kingdom, would constitute an offence of genocide, a crime against humanity or a war crime.[64]

The offence is committed within the territory of the issuing state

8.40   Where the conduct that constitutes the extradition offence occurred within the territory of the issuing state, the territorial conditions that must be satisfied before a court in England and Wales may order extradition of the requested person to the issuing state are:

(1)   the conduct would constitute an offence under the law of England and Wales if it occurred in England and Wales; or

(2)   the conduct:

---

[62]   The relevant sections are s 64 (person not sentenced for offence) and s 65 (person sentenced for the offence). In addition to territorial conditions, s 65 also contain conditions that relate to the sentence passed on the requested person by the issuing state. For the purposes of this report, it is not necessary to refer to those conditions.

[63]   Eg, murder or manslaughter committed by a British citizen – Offences against the Person Act 1861, s 9.

[64]   These are offences against s 51 or s 58 of the International Criminal Court Act 2001.

(a)   constitutes a framework list offence; and

(b)   no part of the conduct occurred in the United Kingdom.

8.41   In *Office of the King's Prosecutor, Brussels v Cando Armas*,[65] the House of Lords held that references to conduct occurring in the territory of the issuing state included conduct occurring wholly *or partly* within the territory of the issuing state. In doing so, the House of Lords recognised the frequency of offences being committed across national borders.

---

[65]   [2005] UKHL 67; [2006] 1 All ER 647.

PART 9
LIST OF RECOMMENDATIONS

9.1 We recommend that there should be two statutory inchoate offences:

(1) encouraging or assisting the commission of a criminal act *intending* that the criminal act should be committed ("the clause 1 offence"), and

(2) encouraging or assisting the commission of a criminal act *believing* that the encouragement or assistance will encourage or assist the commission of the criminal act and believing that the criminal act will be committed ("the clause 2(1) offence"). (Paragraph 5.4)

9.2 We recommend that If the prosecution can prove that D must either have perpetrated the clause 1 or the clause 2(1) offence, on the one hand, or encouraged or assisted its commission, on the other, D can be convicted of the clause 1 or the clause 2(1) offence. (Paragraph 5.11)

9.3 We recommend that the conduct element of both the clause 1 offence and the clause 2(1) offence should consist of *"do[ing] an act capable of encouraging or assisting the doing of a criminal act"*. (Paragraph 5.22)

9.4 We recommend that the doing of an act capable of encouraging or assisting the doing of a criminal act should include doing so by threatening or pressurising another person to do a criminal act. (Paragraph 5.43)

9.5 We recommend that doing an act capable of encouraging or assisting a person to do a criminal act should include doing so by failing to take reasonable steps to discharge a duty. (Paragraph 5.65)

9.6 We recommend that a person failing to respond to a constable's request for assistance in preventing a breach of the peace should not be regarded as the doing of an act capable of encouraging or assisting a person to do a criminal act. (Paragraph 5.67)

9.7 We recommend that in relation to the criminal act of the principal offence, D:

(1) in order to be guilty of the clause 1 offence, must intend[1] that the criminal act should be done or that a person be encouraged or assisted to do it;

(2) in order to be guilty of the clause 2(1) offence, D, although not having to intend that the criminal act should be done, must believe that the criminal act will be done and that his or her own act will encourage or assist the doing of the criminal act. (Paragraph 5.89)

9.8 We recommend that, if D does an act capable of encouraging or assisting the doing of one or more of a number of criminal acts, D must believe:

---

[1] In the sense of what is usually referred to as "direct" intention. See clause 18 of the Bill and Appendix A paras A.26 to A.30 and para A.100.

(1) that at least one of those acts will be done but without having any belief as to which it will be; and

(2) that his or her conduct will encourage or assist the doing of at least one of those acts. (Paragraph 5.94)

9.9 We recommend that if D does an act capable of encouraging or assisting the doing of one or more of a number of criminal acts and D believes:

(1) that at least one of a number of criminal acts will be done but has no belief as to which it will be; and

(2) that his or her act will encourage or assist the doing of at least one of those criminal acts

D may be prosecuted for only one offence. (Paragraph 5.96)

9.10 We recommend that, in order for D to be convicted of the clause 1 or a clause 2 offence:

(1) D must believe that, were another person to do the criminal act, that person would do it with the fault required for conviction of the principal offence; or

(2) D's state of mind must be such that, were he or she to do the criminal act, he or she would do it with that fault. D is to be assumed to be able to do the criminal act in question. (Paragraph 5.105)

9.11 We recommend that if, in addition to a criminal act, a circumstance element or a consequence element, or both, must be proved for conviction of the principal offence, D, in order to be convicted of the clause 1 or a clause 2 offence:

(1) must intend that the criminal act be done in those circumstances or with those consequences; or

(2) must believe that, were the criminal act to be done, it would be done in those circumstances or with those consequences. (Paragraph 5.118)

9.12 We recommend that for committing the clause 1 or a clause 2, D should be liable:

(1) if the principal offence is murder, to imprisonment for life; and

(2) in any other case, unless an enactment provides otherwise, to any penalty for which D would be liable on conviction of the principal offence. (Paragraph 5.127)

9.13 We recommend that the mode of trial in the case of the clause 1 or a clause 2 offence should be determined as if D had been charged with the principal offence. (Paragraph 5.128)

9.14 We recommend that it should be a defence to a charge under clause 1 or clause 2 if D proves that:

(1) he or she acted for the purpose of:

(a)   preventing the commission of either the offence that he or she was encouraging or assisting or another offence; or

(b)   to prevent or limit the occurrence of harm; and

(2)   it was reasonable to act as D did in the circumstances. (Paragraph 6.16)

9.15   We recommend that it should be a defence to a charge under clause 2 if D proves that his or her conduct was reasonable in the circumstances as he knew or reasonably believed them to be. (Paragraph 6.26)

9.16   We recommend that it should be a defence to a charge under clause 1 or clause 2 if:

(1)   the offence encouraged or assisted is one that exists wholly or in part for the protection of a particular category of persons;

(2)   D falls within the protected category;

(3)   D is the person in respect of whom the offence encouraged or assisted was committed or would have been had it had been committed. (Paragraph 6.44)

9.17   We recommend that D may commit the clause 1 offence but not a clause 2 offence by:

(1)   doing an act capable of encouraging or assisting P to do an act capable of encouraging or assisting X to commit an offence , and

(2)   intending that P should do, or be encouraged to do, the act. (paragraph 7.16)

9.18   We recommend that D may commit the clause 1 offence but not a clause 2 offence by:

(1)   doing an act capable of encouraging or assisting X and P to conspire to commit an offence; and

(2)   intending that X and P should conspire, or be encouraged to conspire, to commit the offence. (Paragraph 7.21)

9.19   We recommend that D may commit the clause 1 offence but not a clause 2 offence by:

(1)   doing an act capable of encouraging or assisting P to attempt to commit an offence; and

(2)   intending that P should attempt, or be encouraged to attempt, to commit the offence. (Paragraph 7.24)

9.20   We recommend that D should be guilty of one of the new offences if D knew or believed that the principal offence might be committed wholly or partly in England and Wales, irrespective of where D did the act capable of encouraging or assisting the commission of the principal offence. (Paragraph 8.18)

9.21 We recommend that D may commit one of the new offences if :

(1) D does an act wholly or partly within the jurisdiction capable of encouraging or assisting a person to commit what would be a principal offence under the law of England and Wales;

(2) D knows or believes that the principal offence might be committed wholly or partly in a place outside the jurisdiction;

(3) the principal offence is also an offence under the law of the territory where D knows or believes that it might wholly or partly take place. (Paragraph 8.22)

9.22 We recommend that D may commit one of the new offences if:

(1) D does an act wholly or partly within the jurisdiction capable of encouraging or assisting a person to commit a principal offence under the law of England and Wales;

(2) D knows or believes that the principal offence might be committed wholly or partly in a place outside the jurisdiction;

(3) the principal offence, if committed in that place, is an offence for which the perpetrator could be tried in England and Wales (if he or she satisfies a relevant citizenship, nationality or residence condition, if any). (Paragraph 8.24)

9.23 We recommend that D may commit one of the new offences if:

(1) D's conduct takes place wholly outside the jurisdiction;

(2) D knows or believes that the principal offence might be committed wholly or partly in a place outside the jurisdiction;

(3) D could be tried in England and Wales if he or she committed the principal act in that place. (Paragraph 8.26)

9.24 We recommend that, in cases where it cannot be proved that D knew or believed that the principal offence might take place wholly or partly within the jurisdiction, no proceedings may be instituted except by or with the consent of the Attorney General. (Paragraph 8.28)

(Signed)   ROGER TOULSON, *Chairman*
HUGH BEALE
STUART BRIDGE
JEREMY HORDER
KENNETH PARKER

STEVE HUMPHREYS, *Chief Executive*

24 May 2006

APPENDIX A
COMMENTARY TO THE CRIME
(ENCOURAGING AND ASSISTING) BILL

INTRODUCTION

A.1   In this commentary we explain the various provisions in our draft Crime (Encouraging and Assisting) Bill ("the Bill") and illustrate how they will work. The text of the draft Bill begins on page 144.

PART 1: THE OFFENCES OF ENCOURAGING OR ASSISTING CRIME

Introduction

A.2   Clauses 1(1) and 2(1) set out, respectively, new inchoate offences of "intentionally encouraging or assisting a criminal act" and "encouraging or assisting [a criminal act] believing that [it] will be done".[1] The common law offence of incitement is abolished.[2]

A.3   The new offences are inchoate offences because the encourager or assister ("D") may be liable whether or not the person he believes he is encouraging or assisting goes on to commit the "principal offence" D intends or expects to be committed.[3] For this reason the fault requirement for each of the offences is defined narrowly, with additional safeguards in clauses 2(5) and 5 to limit the reach of the clause 2(1) offence.

A.4   This Bill makes no changes to the common law doctrine of secondary liability. In any case where the principal offence is committed by a perpetrator ("P"), D may be liable for that offence as a secondary party – if he acted with the fault necessary for such liability and provided P with encouragement or assistance – but he may also be liable under Part 1 of the Bill in relation to the criminal act he intended or expected to be committed.[4]

A.5   The fact that the principal offence is committed by P does not affect D's inchoate liability under Part 1 of the Bill. In cases where the principal offence is committed, but D is charged under Part 1 of the Bill, D is liable in relation to the (hypothetical) criminal act he intended or expected, rather than the actual offence committed by P. This will be the position even if the offence committed by P is the same in all respects as the principal offence in relation to which D is charged under Part 1. Accordingly, it is not necessary to include provisions in the Bill to take into account matters such as a change in the way the offence was committed, or a change in the identity of the perpetrator or victim.

---

[1]   Clause 2(2) sets out an additional offence which can most easily be understood once the offence in cl 2(1) has been explained.

[2]   Clause 13. The various *statutory* offences of incitement are unaffected by the Bill.

[3]   Clause 3(1).

[4]   We are working towards producing a draft Bill on secondary liability and innocent agency in the near future.

A.6   In paragraphs A.8 to A.22 we explain the common actus reus (external element) of the two offences created by clauses 1(1) and 2(1). We then focus on the additional requirements for liability under clause 1(1) (paragraphs A.26 to A.43) and clause 2(1) (paragraphs A.44 to A.50 and A.54).

A.7   Clause 2(2), covering a particular type of encouraging or assisting which is related to, but different from, the situation covered by clause 2(1), is explained in paragraphs A.51 to A.54.

Clauses 1(1) and 2(1): the common "actus reus"

A.8   To be liable for any criminal offence a perpetrator must commit its "actus reus", the traditional label for the external aspect of an offence comprising one or more of the following elements: conduct, circumstances and consequence.

A.9   The actus reus is the same for both clause 1(1) and clause 2(1).[5] In other words, the difference between the way the two offences are defined relates to the mental element (the culpable state of mind the Crown must prove D had). Clause 1(1) requires proof of an intention to encourage or assist another person to do a relevant criminal act.[6] Clause 2(1) requires proof that D believed that another person would do a relevant criminal act with his encouragement or assistance.[7]

A.10   The common actus reus for liability under Part 1 of the Bill is an act (or a failure to take reasonable steps to discharge a duty to act)[8] which is "capable of encouraging or assisting the doing of a criminal act".[9]

A.11   In most cases this means that D must do something capable of encouraging or assisting another person to do something which could fall within the definition of the conduct element of the principal offence in question, without reference to the principal offence's circumstance or consequence elements (if any).[10] Reference is made to the circumstance and consequence elements (if any) in the provisions defining D's fault.[11]

A.12   We can take the principal offences of rape and murder as examples:

---

5   See cl 1(1)(a) and cl 2(1)(a).

6   Clause 1(1)(b).

7   Clause 2(1)(b).

8   See cl 15(2)(b). In this commentary references to D's doing something or to his conduct should be taken to include references to his being in breach of a duty to do something.

9   Clause 1(1)(a) and cl 2(1)(a).

10   Clause 17(2) explains that a principal offence's "criminal act" is a reference to "an act (or a failure to act) that falls within the definition of the act (or failure to act) that must be proved in order for a person [P] to be convicted of the offence".

11   Clause 1(2)–(3) and cl 2(3)–(4).

D will commit the actus reus of the two offences in relation to rape if D's conduct could encourage or assist a man to penetrate (or continue to penetrate)[12] another person with his penis (the conduct element of rape);[13]

D will commit the actus reus of the two offences in relation to murder if D's conduct could encourage or assist a person to do (or continue to do) something which, if done against another person, could cause that person's death (the conduct element of murder).

A.13   Section 1(1)(a) of the Sexual Offences Act 2003 defines the conduct element of rape so that it encompasses only three types of sexual penetration.

A.14   The conduct element of murder, by contrast, can be committed in a wide range of different ways (for example, by firing a loaded gun at someone, pushing someone under a moving car, giving someone a poisoned apple, stabbing someone in the heart, dropping a concrete slab on someone's head, and so on).

A.15   Accordingly, whereas D will commit the actus reus of clause 1(1) and clause 2(1) in relation to rape only if his conduct could have encouraged or assisted one or more of three types of sexual penetration, D will commit the actus reus of clause 1(1) and clause 2(1) in relation to murder if his conduct could have encouraged or assisted another person to do any act which, if done against a person, could have resulted in a person's death.

A.16   It should not be thought, however, that the actus reus can be committed only in cases where the assistance has a direct bearing on the commission of the criminal act in question. Assistance may also be provided in a less direct sense, for example by the provision of accommodation (such as the room where the rape is expected to take place) or a service (such as driving P to the place where it is believed he will commit murder).

A.17   Although the term "criminal act" will usually be taken to be a reference to the conduct element of the principal offence, as explained above, the term will occasionally need to be construed more widely so that it encompasses the offence's circumstance element. This broader construction will be necessary if the conduct element of the principal offence is nothing more than a neutral setting for the principal offence in terms of what might be encouraged or assisted.

---

[12]   Clause 17(3)(a).

[13]   Sexual Offences Act 2003, s 1(1)(a). Lack of consent is the circumstance element of rape.

A.18   An obvious example is the offence of "drink-driving".[14] If D, knowing or believing that some other person (P) will soon be driving home, encourages or assists him to drink copious amounts of whisky, it would not be possible to say that D's conduct has the capacity to encourage or assist P to commit the conduct element of the offence (that is, the driving). D's behaviour does, however, have the capacity to encourage or assist P to be intoxicated (the circumstance element) or to be intoxicated while driving (the combination of conduct and circumstance elements).[15]

A.19   For principal offences of this type, we expect the courts to interpret the term "criminal act" so that it comprises the combination of conduct and circumstance elements. Thus, to take again the example of "drink-driving", so long as D acts with the required fault, he will be liable for encouraging or assisting a person to commit that offence if his conduct has the capacity to encourage or assist another person to drive on a road while over the limit.

A.20   It is important to note that, whatever the nature of the principal offence in question, D's conduct need only have the *capacity* to encourage or assist the "criminal act" of the intended or expected offence. No actual encouragement or assistance is required for liability under clause 1(1) or clause 2(1) because the principal offence may never be committed. Indeed, it may be that no-one (or no-one other than D) ever intended that it should be committed. Thus, to be liable under clause 1(1) or clause 2(1), D need only do something which *could* have encouraged or assisted a person (on the assumption that that person would go on to do the act D intended or expected).

A.21   It follows that, although there must always be some form of conduct on the part of D for him to be liable under Part 1 of the Bill, that conduct may be ostensibly innocent when observed without reference to D's own (culpable) state of mind. As with some other offences, particularly the inchoate offence of attempt,[16] it is primarily D's state of mind which determines whether he is criminally liable for his conduct.

A.22   For example, if D hands a jemmy over to P, in the belief that P will commit burglary by using the jemmy to effect his entry into a building,[17] D will be liable under clause 2(1) for encouraging or assisting burglary, regardless of P's own intentions. However, D would not be liable under clause 2(1) if he delivered the jemmy to P for an entirely innocent reason, anticipating no crime, even though the jemmy had the capacity to assist burglary and was in fact subsequently used by P to commit that offence.

A.23   An act of encouraging is of course less likely than an act of assisting to appear innocent when viewed without reference to D's state of mind. Indeed, in cases of encouraging it will often be possible to infer D's culpable state of mind from his conduct.

---

[14]   Road Traffic Act 1988, s 5(1)(a).

[15]   Other examples are speeding, dangerous driving and being drunk and disorderly.

[16]   Criminal Attempts Act 1981, s 1.

[17]   Theft Act 1968, s 9(1)(a).

A.24   Because clauses 1 and 2[18] define inchoate offences, it is necessary to ensure that they do not have too wide a reach. This is particularly true in relation to clause 2, which imposes criminal liability on "indifferent" encouragers and assisters.[19]

A.25   Accordingly, clauses 4 and 6 provide limitations on the scope of clauses 1 and 2, clause 5 provides D with a special "reasonableness" defence if he is charged under clause 2, and clause 2(5) limits the range of principal offences to which clause 2 can be applied.

Clause 1 – intentionally encouraging or assisting a criminal act

A.26   In order to be convicted of an offence under clause 1(1), the Crown must also prove that D had the required intention, that is, that he acted with a particular purpose.[20]

A.27   The intention requirement has been drafted so that D must intend to encourage or assist a person to commit the conduct element of the principal offence.[21] This definition is broad enough to cover two types of intention. It covers the typical case where D's purpose is to see the conduct element of the principal offence committed; but it is also wide enough to encompass a case such as the following:

> D, a wholesaler for career criminals, encourages a customer (P) to commit burglary in order to persuade him to purchase expensive cutting equipment. D's purpose is to encourage P to commit burglary, but he is indifferent as to the commission of that principal offence.

A.28   Clause 1(1)(b) is *not* wide enough, however, to cover the situation where D's only purpose is to do an act which, incidentally, he knows or believes will encourage or assist another person to commit an offence. For example:

> D, an ironmonger, intentionally sells a piece of lead piping to a customer (P), believing that P will use it to commit murder.

---

[18] As explained in n 1, cl 2 contains two offences, defined by cl 2(1) and cl 2(2).

[19] D is "indifferent" because he does not act with the intention required for liability under cl 1(1). Rather, D believes, or knows, that an offence will be committed or is in the process of being committed.

[20] In this context intention does not include foresight of the consequences of one's conduct (see cl 18).

[21] Clause 1(1)(b) with cl 17(2). Of course, if the principal offence is one of the exceptional offences having a neutral conduct element (in terms of what can be encouraged or assisted), so that the term "criminal act" must include a reference to the combination of conduct and circumstances, then D must intend to encourage or assist the doing of that conduct in those circumstances (see paras A.17 to A.19 above).

A.29   In this situation D would not incur liability under clause 1(1) for intentionally encouraging or assisting murder as his only purpose is to effect a sale and make a profit, albeit in the belief that murder will be committed with the item sold. It is not D's purpose to provide encouragement or assistance in relation to any conduct which could cause death. In other words, clause 1(1) does not encompass individuals such as the "indifferent" shopkeeper or householder who sells or lends an item in the belief that it will be used to achieve a particular criminal end.[22]

A.30   The application of clause 1(1) may be illustrated with reference, again, to the principal offences of murder and rape:

> For D to be liable under clause 1(1) for intentionally encouraging or assisting murder, it will be necessary for the Crown to prove that it was D's purpose to encourage or assist a person to commit the conduct element of murder.[23] It will not be necessary for the Crown to prove that it was D's purpose that a person should be killed.[24]
>
> For D to be liable under clause 1(1) for intentionally encouraging or assisting rape, the Crown will have to prove that it was D's purpose to encourage or assist a man to commit the conduct element of rape.[25] It will not be necessary for the Crown to prove that D's purpose extended to the complainant's lack of consent.[26]

A.31   However, this does not mean that no culpable state of mind is required with respect to the circumstance and consequence elements of the principal offence. In addition to the requirement of intention described above, the Crown must also prove (where applicable) that:

  (1)   D believed that, if the conduct element of the principal offence were to be committed, it would be committed by a person acting with the fault required for liability as a perpetrator (or D himself acted with such fault);[27] and

  (2)   D believed that the conduct element, if committed, would be committed in the circumstances and with the consequences required for the principal offence to be committed (or D intended that the conduct element should be done in those circumstances with those consequences).[28]

---

[22]   However, it will be seen below that individuals of this sort may be guilty of the inchoate offence created by cl 2(1).

[23]   See paras A.12 and A.14 above.

[24]   The consequence element of murder.

[25]   Defined in s 1(1)(a) of the Sexual Offences Act 2003.

[26]   The circumstance element of rape.

[27]   Clause 1(2). The alternative in cl 1(2)(b) – D acts with the fault for the principal offence – means that D can be liable under cl 1(1) if his state of mind is that of a person who commits the principal offence through an innocent agent. Where cl 1(2)(b) is relied on, it is to be assumed that D is able to do the criminal act in question (cl 11).

[28]   Clause 1(3). The first of these two alternatives is found in cl 1(3)(b); the second alternative, summarised here in parentheses, is found in cl 1(3)(a).

A.32   The requirement set out in paragraph A.31(1), summarising clause 1(2), applies only to principal offences with a fault element, whether that fault element has been defined in "subjective" terms (that is, by reference to the perpetrator's state of mind) or in "objective" terms (that is, by reference to the state of mind of a reasonable person) or both.[29]

A.33   Thus, subject to the additional requirements of clause 1(3) being satisfied:

> D would be liable under clause 1(1) in relation to murder if he intends to encourage or assist a person to commit the conduct element of murder and believes that, were a person to commit that conduct element, he would do so with the intention to kill or cause grievous bodily harm;

> D would be liable under clause 1(1) in relation to rape if he intends to encourage or assist a person to commit the conduct element of rape (any of three types of sexual penetration) and believes that, were a person to commit that conduct element, he would do so without a reasonable belief that his victim is consenting[30] (and with the intention to penetrate).[31]

A.34   For most principal offences with a fault requirement, the definition of that fault will relate to the consequence and circumstance elements of the offence's actus reus. Accordingly, because under clause 1(2) D must have belief in relation to the fault of an anticipated perpetrator, it is likely that D will also have belief in relation to the occurrence of the consequence and circumstance elements of the principal offence for the purposes of clause 1(3).[32]

A.35   The requirements of clause 1(3) are set out in paragraph A.31(2). This provision is of particular importance if the principal offence is:

(1)   a "no fault" offence; or

(2)   an offence requiring proof of fault which has a consequence and/or circumstance element, but no fault requirement in relation to one or both of those elements.[33]

A.36   Where the principal offence has no requirement of fault, D's liability for intentionally encouraging or assisting the commission of the offence is governed by clause 1(3) rather than clause 1(2). For example:

---

[29]   In other words, cl 1(2) applies to all principal offences which are not "no fault" offences.

[30]   Sexual Offences Act 2003, s 1(1)(c).

[31]   Sexual Offences Act 2003, s 1(1)(a). It may be that the "intentionally penetrates" requirement falls outside the definition of fault. See n 34 below.

[32]   Clause 1(3)(b).

[33]   An example is murder (see para A.37).

For D to be liable for intentionally encouraging or assisting the no fault offence of child rape, contrary to section 5 of the Sexual Offences Act 2003,[34] D must believe that, if the intended conduct element of rape were to be committed by another person, the victim would be under the age of 13[35] (or D must intend that the conduct element of rape should be committed against a child under the age of 13).[36]

A.37 Both clause 1(2) and clause 1(3) apply if the offence is defined with a requirement of fault but, as noted above, clause 1(3) is particularly important if the actus reus of the principal offence has a consequence or circumstance element to which the fault requirement does not relate. Murder is an offence of this sort because the actus reus requires the death of a human being (the consequence element) but the fault requirement can be satisfied by an intention to cause nothing more than grievous bodily harm.

A.38 Consider the following variations of a broadly similar factual scenario:

> P approaches D and asks if he can borrow D's baseball bat. P says he intends to use the bat to "sort out V". D provides P with the bat, unclear as to P's exact intention but hoping that P will use it to cause V serious harm. P does nothing with the bat.

> P approaches D and asks if he can borrow D's baseball bat. P says he intends to use the bat to "sort out V". D provides P with the bat, unclear as to P's exact intention but hoping that P will use it to kill V. P does nothing with the bat.

A.39 In the first version, D is not liable under clause 1(1) for intentionally encouraging or assisting murder, even though he would have acted with the fault for murder if he himself had committed the conduct element of that offence.[37] Although clause 1(2) is satisfied, clause 1(3) is not because D does not believe that V will be killed[38] (and it was not D's purpose that V should be killed).[39]

---

[34] The likelihood is that s 5 of the 2003 Act will be regarded as a no fault offence, notwithstanding the reference in s 5(1)(a) to intentional penetration by P. In this context, the word "intentionally" is likely to be regarded as a reference to the concept of volition (part of the actus reus of the offence) rather than an element of fault. (If the allegation is one of attempt, however, it will be necessary to prove the intention to penetrate in accordance with the terms of s 1(1) of the Criminal Attempts Act 1981.)

[35] Clause 1(3)(b)(i).

[36] Clause 1(3)(a)(i).

[37] Clause 1(2)(b). D is, however, liable for intentionally encouraging or assisting the offence of causing grievous bodily harm with intent (Offences Against the Person Act 1861, s 18).

[38] Clause 1(3)(b)(ii).

[39] Clause 1(3)(a)(ii).

A.40   In the second version, however, D is liable for the offence of intentionally encouraging or assisting murder. By providing P with a baseball bat, D commits the actus reus, that is, he does an act capable of assisting another person to commit the conduct element of murder.[40] With regard to the fault requirement: D intended to assist P to commit the conduct element of that offence (indeed he intended that the conduct element should be committed);[41] D's state of mind was such that, if he had killed V himself, he would have been liable for murder as a perpetrator;[42] and it was his purpose that a person (V) should die.[43]

A.41   Clause 1(1) will of course be relied on in cases where the principal offence is not committed. But it will also be relied on in cases where the principal offence *is* committed but the Crown cannot prove that the perpetrator (P) was actually encouraged or assisted by D's conduct for the doctrine of secondary liability to bite.[44] Consider the following examples:

> D distributes a leaflet encouraging acts of extreme violence against individuals who have a particular political affiliation. D's purpose is to encourage his readers to commit such acts, so that one or more acts of extreme violence will be committed.

> D enters P's bedroom to find him engaged in sexual intercourse with V. D knows that V is not consenting, and that P is aware of this, but he nevertheless positions himself in front of P to watch, intending to encourage P by his being there. P continues to rape V, aware that D is watching, but he is not influenced by D's presence to any extent.

A.42   In the first example, D is liable under clause 1(1) in relation to the principal offence of causing grievous bodily harm with intent,[45] even if no one from the targeted party is ever attacked. Under our proposals for secondary liability,[46] D would be liable for the completed offence of causing grievous bodily harm with intent if that offence is subsequently committed by a person (P) who has read and been encouraged by D's leaflet.

---

[40] Clause 1(1)(a). See paras A.12 and A.14 above.

[41] Clause 1(1)(b).

[42] Clause 1(2)(b).

[43] Clause 1(3)(a)(ii).

[44] Proof of actual encouragement or assistance would seem to be necessary at common law, and it will be required under our forthcoming proposals for reforming the doctrine.

[45] Offences Against the Person Act 1861, s 18.

[46] In line with the common law doctrine in this respect.

A.43   In the second example, although P is wholly unaffected by D's presence, D is liable under clause 1(1) in relation to the principal offence of rape.[47] By positioning himself in front of P, D has done something capable of encouraging a person to commit the conduct element of rape;[48] D's purpose is to encourage a person to commit the conduct element of rape;[49] and D believes that, if the conduct element continues, it will be continued by a person acting with the fault for rape[50] (that is, the absence of a reasonable belief that V is consenting) in the circumstances (that is, without consent) necessary for rape to be committed.[51] Under our proposals for secondary liability, D would be liable for the completed offence of rape if P was encouraged by D's presence.

A.44   Finally, with regard to principal offences which have a circumstance element, clause 1 also encompasses the type of situation where D intentionally encourages or assists a person to do the offence's criminal act but he does not care whether the circumstance element is present. For example, if D orders P to have sexual intercourse with V "whether she consents or not", D is liable for intentionally encouraging or assisting rape because D believes that, if P were to have sexual intercourse with V, P "would do it" in the circumstances[52] and with the fault[53] required for rape should V refuse to consent.

Clause 2 – encouraging or assisting criminal acts believing that one or more of them will be done

A.45   Clause 2(1) sets out the second basis for inchoate liability for encouraging or assisting crime under Part 1 of the Bill, defined in terms of D's belief rather than his purpose. As explained above,[54] D can be liable under clause 2(1) only if he does an act which is capable of encouraging or assisting another person to do a "criminal act" in relation to the principal offence he believes will be committed.[55] It is irrelevant whether or not the principal offence is ever committed.[56]

---

[47]   Sexual Offences Act 2003, s 1.

[48]   Clause 1(1)(a).

[49]   Clause 1(1)(b).

[50]   Clause 1(2)(a).

[51]   Clause 1(3)(b)(i).

[52]   Clause 1(3)(b).

[53]   Clause 1(2)(a).

[54]   Paras A.8 to A.22.

[55]   Clause 2(1)(a) and cl 17(2). Clause 2(1)(a) provides that D must do an act capable of encouraging or assisting the doing of a criminal act (the "act in question"). Clause 2(6) provides that the "principal offence" is the offence in relation to which the "act in question" is a criminal act.

[56]   Clause 3(1).

A.46   If the principal offence *is* committed by P, under our proposals for secondary liability an "indifferent" encourager or assister[57] (D) would be liable for P's principal offence only if he was a participant in a joint venture to commit an offence, and he foresaw the possible commission of the principal offence in furtherance of the venture.[58] In other circumstances, indifferent encouragers or assisters acting with the required belief would be convicted of the clause 2(1) offence in relation to the anticipated offence. They would not be secondarily liable for the offence actually committed by P.

A.47   The fault element for liability under clause 2(1) can be broken down as follows, for offences defined with a requirement of fault:[59]

   (1)   D believes that another person will commit the conduct element of the principal offence in question;[60]

   (2)   D believes that his own conduct will encourage or assist a person to commit the conduct element of the principal offence;[61] and

   (3)   D believes that the conduct element of the principal offence, if committed, will be committed by a person acting with the fault required for the principal offence (or D himself acts with such fault)[62] in the circumstances and with the consequences, if any, required for the principal offence to be committed.[63]

A.48   Given that clause 2 defines the parameters for inchoate liability, we expect the words "will" and "would" to be interpreted narrowly. In particular, D would not be liable under this clause if he merely believed that the principal offence might be committed.

A.49   Consider the following two examples:

   P calls on D, his neighbour, and asks if he can borrow D's baseball bat, expressing his wish to give V a severe beating. D is indifferent to V's fate, but lends the bat to P to maintain good neighbourly relations.

---

[57]   "Indifferent" because it is not D's purpose to encourage or assist another person to commit (the conduct element of) the offence in question.

[58]   The present common law doctrine is wider, encompassing indifferent encouragers and assisters who are not involved in a joint venture to commit an offence.

[59]   Clause 2(1)(b) and cl 2(3)–(4) (read with cl 17(2)) For principal offences having no fault requirement, cl 2(3) is irrelevant.

[60]   Clause 2(1)(b)(i). This is satisfied if D believes that a person will commit the conduct element only if one or more conditions are satisfied (cl 3(5)). For example, D may be liable under cl 2(1) for knowingly encouraging or assisting murder, by providing P with an empty gun, if he believes that P will obtain ammunition for it from another source.

[61]   Clause 2(1)(b)(ii).

[62]   Clause 2(3). The alternative in cl 2(3)(b) – D acts with the fault for the principal offence – means that D can be liable under cl 2(1) if his state of mind, in this context, is that of a person who commits the principal offence through an innocent agent. Where cl 2(3)(b) is relied on, it is to be assumed that D is able to do the criminal act in question (cl 11).

[63]   Clause 2(4).

D, the inventor, manufacturer or wholesaler of equipment designed to reverse the flow of current through electricity meters, supplies one such "black box" to another person in the belief that it will be used by him (or the end-user) to divert electricity to avoid having to pay for it.

A.50   In the first example, D is liable under clause 2(1) for the offence of knowingly encouraging or assisting the principal offence of causing grievous bodily harm with intent ("the section 18 offence"),[64] whether or not P goes on to commit the section 18 offence. D's conduct in lending his baseball bat is an act capable of assisting another person (P) to commit the conduct element of the section 18 offence,[65] D believes that P will use the bat to commit the conduct element of that offence,[66] D believes that P will act with the fault required for such liability[67] (that is, the intention to cause serious harm)[68] and D believes that P will, by his conduct, cause the required consequence for section 18 liability (that is, serious harm).[69]

A.51   In the second example, D is liable for the offence of encouraging or assisting the offence of abstracting electricity[70] because he does something capable of assisting a person to commit the conduct element of that offence;[71] he believes that someone will commit the conduct element[72] (and that his "black box" will provide assistance);[73] and he believes that, if a person commits the conduct element, he will do so with the required fault (that is, dishonestly)[74] and cause electricity to be abstracted.[75]

---

[64]   Offences Against the Person Act 1861, s 18.

[65]   Clause 2(1)(a).

[66]   Clause 2(1)(b)(i)–(ii).

[67]   Clause 2(3)(a).

[68]   Section 18 of the Offences Against the Person Act 1861 is defined with alternative requirements of fault, one of which is the intention to cause grievous (that is, serious) bodily harm.

[69]   Clause 2(4)(b).

[70]   Theft Act 1968, s 13.

[71]   Clause 2(1)(a). The conduct element of this offence is any act which could lead to the consequence of electricity being used, wasted or diverted.

[72]   Clause 2(1)(b)(i).

[73]   Clause 2(1)(b)(ii).

[74]   Clause 2(3)(a).

[75]   Clause 2(4)(b). This situation is now covered by the common law offence of conspiracy to defraud (see *Hollinshead* [1985] 1 AC 975, where D supplied an undercover police officer with such "black boxes"). We recommended the abolition of conspiracy to defraud in our Report on Fraud, Law Com No 276 at pp 83–84, accepting that this could create a lacuna in cases where a person *assisted* in a fraud (p 100, n 14). The cl 2(1) offence of encouraging or assisting a crime would address this lacuna should conspiracy to defraud be abolished. It would also cover the type of situation addressed in n 15 of p 101 of our Report on Fraud, where D is an assister on the fringe of a conspiracy, but does not know the details of what the protagonists are planning. D would be liable under cl 2(1) on the basis of the offence he anticipated, regardless of what anyone else intended to do.

A.52 Clause 2(2) addresses the specific problem where D's conduct has the capacity to provide another person with encouragement or assistance in relation to a range of possible principal offences,[76] and D believes that one of the offences in that range will be committed (with his encouragement or assistance) but he is unclear which offence it will be.[77] It is the type of situation which arose (in the context of secondary liability) in *DPP for Northern Ireland v Maxwell*.[78] The following factual scenario provides an example:

> D, a taxi driver, is asked by a group of armed men to drive to a public house in the East End of London. D believes that they *will* commit an offence of violence and, from their comments to each other, he concludes that the offence *might* be robbery or it *might* be causing grievous bodily harm with intent.

A.53 In a case of this sort, the Crown will prosecute D under clause 2(2) in relation to just one of the possible principal offences he believed might be committed,[79] such as the offence of robbery in the above example. D may, however, be prosecuted in the same proceedings under clause 2(1) and clause 2(2) if the requirements of both subsections are met,[80] as in the following example:

> D, a taxi driver, drives a group of armed men to a public house believing that they *will* commit robbery (clause 2(1)) and also believing that they *will* commit an additional offence against the landlord which *might* be causing him actual bodily harm or causing him grievous bodily harm with intent (clause 2(2)).

A.54 To be liable under clause 2(2) in relation to the selected principal offence the fault requirements in clause 2(3) (for principal offences requiring proof of fault) and clause 2(4) must also be proved.

A.55 Finally, clause 2(5) provides that D cannot be liable under clause 2(1) or clause 2(2) in relation to either of those offences, or the clause 1(1) offence, or any of the offences listed in Schedule 1 to the Bill. The list of offences in Schedule 1 includes the statutory forms of incitement, the inchoate offences of attempt and conspiracy and the offences of post-offence assisting in sections 4(1) and 5(1) of the Criminal Law Act 1967.

Clause 3 – supplemental provisions

A.56 Much of clause 3 has already been explained.[81] In other respects, the clause is self-explanatory.

---

[76] Clause 2(2)(a).

[77] Clause 2(2)(b). By virtue of cl 3(6) D is to be taken to believe that at least one criminal act will be done if he believes that one will be done if certain conditions are met.

[78] [1978] 1 WLR 1350.

[79] Clause 3(4).

[80] Clause 3(3).

[81] See n 3 (para A.3), n 56 (para A.45), n 60 (para A.47), n 77 (para A.52), n 79 (para A.53) and n 80 (para A.53).

PART 2: DEFENCES AND LIMITATIONS ON LIABILITY

Clause 4 – the "good purpose" defence

A.57   If the Crown establishes a prima facie case that D is liable under Part 1 of the Bill D will be entitled to an acquittal if he can prove, on the balance of probabilities, that his purpose was to prevent the commission of the principal offence in question (or some other offence) or to prevent or limit the occurrence of harm and that his conduct was reasonable in the circumstances.[82] For example:

> D involves himself in a joint venture to commit burglary. D's defence is that his only purpose in becoming involved was to obtain sufficient information about the offence to be able to inform the police in advance to ensure that the other participants would be caught in the act.

A.58   If the jury accepts that D's explanation is more likely than any other explanation to be true and that it was reasonable for D to act in that way, he will not be guilty under Part 1 in relation to burglary. We would expect this defence to be extended to cover conspiracy (and secondary liability) too in due course.

A.59   If D is charged under clause 1(1), on the basis that his purpose was to encourage or assist a person to commit a criminal act in relation to the principal offence, it may well be difficult for him to discharge the burden of proving that the requirements of the defence are made out, but he is not precluded from relying on the defence. The defence might, for example, be made out in the following situation:

> Having found out that P, a person motivated by his hostility towards a racial group, is considering whether to steal a wallet from or, alternatively, to cause a serious injury to a person belonging to that group, D encourages P to commit the theft.

A.60   D could give evidence in his defence, to a charge under clause 1(1) of intentionally encouraging or assisting theft, that he encouraged P to steal in order to prevent the more serious crime being committed. If the jury accepts that D acted to prevent a serious attack by P on another person, and regard his act of encouragement as a reasonable course of conduct in the circumstances, D will not be guilty of the offence charged.

Clause 5 – the "reasonableness" defence

A.61   This clause provides a limit to the scope of the offence of encouraging or assisting crime contrary to clause 2(1) (or clause 2(2)). It cannot be relied on if D is charged under clause 1(1).

---

[82] The legal burden is on D to *prove* the good purpose *and* that his conduct was reasonable in the circumstances.

A.62   D will not be convicted of the clause 2(1) (or clause 2(2)) offence if, in the circumstances he was aware of,[83] or in the circumstances he reasonably believed existed,[84] it was reasonable for him to act as he did.[85] In each case it will be for the tribunal of fact[86] to decide whether, notwithstanding D's prima facie liability, he ought nevertheless to be acquitted. It is therefore for D to prove that the defence is made out on the balance of probabilities.

A.63   D would no doubt wish to avail himself of the defence against a charge under clause 2(1) arising out of the following scenarios:

>   D, a motorist, changes motorway lanes to allow a following motorist (P) to overtake, even though D knows that P is speeding;

>   D, a reclusive householder, bars his front door to a man trying to get into his house to escape from a prospective assailant (P);

>   D, a member of a DIY shop's check-out staff, believes the man (P) purchasing spray paint will use it to cause criminal damage.

Clause 6 – the "*Tyrrell*" defence

A.64   This clause retains the exemption from liability established at common law in the case of *Tyrrell*.[87] D cannot be liable under Part 1 in relation to a (statutory) "protective" principal offence[88] if he falls within the category of persons the principal offence was enacted to protect[89] and he would be regarded as the "victim" if the offence were committed against him.[90] Consider the following example:

>   D1 (a 12-year-old girl) and D2 (D1's 15-year-old female friend) both encourage a man (P) to have sexual intercourse with D1 (an act which, if committed by P, would amount to the principal offence of child rape).[91]

A.65   On the basis that D1 would be regarded as the "victim" of P's offence, and that Parliament intended section 5 of the Sexual Offences Act 2003 to protect children under the age of 13 from themselves, as well as from predatory adults:

>   (1)   D1 would not be liable under Part 1 of the Bill in relation to the offence of child rape even though it was her purpose to encourage P to have sexual intercourse with her.

---

[83]   Clause 5(1)(a).

[84]   Clause 5(2)(a)–(b).

[85]   Clause 5(1)(b) and cl 5(2)(c).

[86]   The jury for trials on indictment in the Crown Court. The magistrates or district judge for summary trials in magistrates' courts.

[87]   [1894] 1 QB 710.

[88]   Clause 6(1)(a) and cl 6(2).

[89]   Clause 6(1)(b).

[90]   Clause 6(1)(c) explains that the victim is "the person in respect of whom the principal offence was committed (or would have been if it had been committed)".

[91]   Sexual Offences Act 2003, s 5.

(2)   D2 would be liable under clause 1(1) in relation to that principal offence.

A.66   We would expect this defence to be extended to cover conspiracy (and secondary liability) in due course.[92]

PART 3: JURISDICTION AND PROCEDURE

Clauses 7 and 8 with Schedule 2 – jurisdiction

A.67   As a general rule the criminal courts in England and Wales are empowered to convict an offender if the offence in question occurred in England or Wales, but not if the offence was committed elsewhere. The power to convict any particular offender is rarely in issue in criminal proceedings in this jurisdiction because the vast majority of cases tried here relate to offences allegedly committed here. Similarly, we would expect the vast majority of prosecutions brought under this Bill to raise no jurisdictional issues. The Crown's case will usually be that D's relevant conduct occurred, and the anticipated[93] principal offence was expected to occur, wholly within the jurisdictional territory of England and Wales. Nevertheless, because of the multifarious ways in which encouragement or assistance may be provided, and the fact that assistance or encouragement may be sent from, and to, any part of the world, the question of jurisdiction is of particular importance in the context of this Bill.

A.68   Accordingly, clause 7 and Schedule 2 set out a number of rules on jurisdiction (for liability under Part 1 of the Bill) to which the court will refer for any allegation falling outside the usual state of affairs.

A.69   Clause 7(1) sets out the rule that D may be convicted of the Part 1 offences regardless of his own location at any relevant time, if he knew or believed that the anticipated principal offence might be committed wholly or partly in England or Wales.

A.70   This provision therefore allows D to be convicted here in the usual "domestic" situation where his own conduct occurred in England or Wales and he believed that the offence would (or might) also be committed in England or Wales; but it also allows D to be convicted here if his own conduct occurred outside England and Wales if he believed that the offence might be committed wholly or partly in England or Wales. For example:

> D in Afghanistan sends an e-mail to P in Manchester directing him to plant a bomb in central London.

A.71   Clause 7(2) provides that if the Crown cannot prove that D knew or believed that the anticipated principal offence might be committed wholly or partly in England or Wales, he may be convicted of the offences in Part 1 only if the facts fall within paragraph 1, 2 or 3 of Schedule 2.

A.72   Clause 8 provides, in addition, that where Schedule 2 is relied on the proceedings must be instituted by, or with the consent of, the Attorney General.

---

[92]   It should be noted that the *Tyrrell* defence in cl 6 is not limited to sexual offences.

[93]   See cl 7(3)–(4).

Schedule 2, paragraph 1

A.73   If the Crown cannot prove that D knew or believed that the anticipated principal offence might be committed wholly or partly in England or Wales, the court has jurisdiction by virtue of paragraph 1 if:

(1)   D's relevant conduct occurred wholly or partly in England or Wales;

(2)   D knew or believed that the anticipated principal offence might occur wholly or partly in a place outside England and Wales; and

(3)   the anticipated principal offence, if committed in that place, is one for which a perpetrator could be convicted in England or Wales (if he satisfies a relevant citizenship or nationality or residence requirement, if any).

A.74   For example:

> D in London sends a parcel of poison to a person in Paris encouraging him to use it to commit murder in Brussels. D can be convicted in England or Wales of the offence of intentionally encouraging or assisting murder because, if murder were to be committed in Brussels, it would be possible to convict the perpetrator in England or Wales if he satisfies the requirement of being a "subject of her Majesty".[94]

> D in London sends a letter to a person in Jakarta encouraging him to commit an act of piracy on the high seas. D can be convicted in England or Wales of the offence of intentionally encouraging or assisting piracy on the high seas because, if piracy were to be committed on the high seas, it would be possible to convict the perpetrator in England or Wales.[95]

Schedule 2, paragraph 2

A.75   If the Crown cannot prove that D knew or believed that the anticipated principal offence might be committed wholly or partly in England or Wales, and paragraph 1 cannot be relied on, the court has jurisdiction by virtue of paragraph 2 if:

(1)   D's relevant conduct occurred wholly or partly in England or Wales;

(2)   D knew or believed that the anticipated principal offence might occur wholly or partly in a place outside England and Wales; and

(3)   the anticipated principal offence,[96] if committed, would also be an offence under the law in force in that place.

A.76   For example:

---

[94]   Offences Against the Person Act 1861, s 9.

[95]   Because piracy on the high seas is a crime against the law of nations, P may be convicted of the offence in any sovereign state.

[96]   An offence in England and Wales.

D in London e-mails P in Brisbane encouraging him to commit robbery while he is in Sydney. D can be convicted in England or Wales of the offence of intentionally encouraging or assisting robbery because robbery is also an offence in New South Wales.

Schedule 2, paragraph 3

A.77 Paragraph 3 provides the court with jurisdiction in the situation where D's relevant conduct took place wholly outside England and Wales (and the Crown cannot prove that D knew or believed that the anticipated principal offence might be committed wholly or partly in England or Wales). In this situation, D may be convicted in England or Wales of an offence in Part 1 if:

(1) D knew or believed that the anticipated principal offence might occur wholly or partly in a place outside England and Wales; and

(2) it would be possible to convict D in England or Wales (as the perpetrator of the principal offence) if he were to commit the principal offence in that place.

A.78 For example:

D (a British citizen) in the Philippines encourages a man to rape a 10-year-old girl in Manila. D can be convicted in England or Wales of an offence of encouraging or assisting child-rape because, as a British citizen, it would be possible to convict D in England or Wales of child-rape if he perpetrated that offence in Manila.[97]

D (a British citizen) in Canada encourages a person to commit murder in Vancouver. D can be convicted in England or Wales of an offence of encouraging or assisting murder because, as a British citizen, it would be possible to convict him in England or Wales of murder if he perpetrated that offence in Canada.[98]

Clause 9 – mode of trial

A.79 This clause is self-explanatory.

Clause 10 – unknown mode of participation

A.80 One of the most important practical aspects of the doctrine of secondary liability is that an accused person may be convicted of an offence if it cannot be proved whether he was a perpetrator or an accessory but it can be proved that he must have been one or the other.

A.81 Clause 10 provides a similar rule, applicable in cases where the principal offence has actually been committed, rendering the accused guilty of an offence under Part 1 of the Bill if it can be proved that he was either a perpetrator or guilty of one of the new inchoate offences but his precise role cannot be proved.

---

[97] Sexual Offences Act 2003, s 72 and sch 2.

[98] Offences Against the Person Act 1861, s 9.

A.82   The following example illustrates how clause 10 could be applied in practice:

> A1 and A2, the parents of an infant child (V), are proved to have been present during the assault which resulted in V's death, and it can be proved that A1 or A2 perpetrated the offence. There is, however, insufficient evidence to convict either or both of them as perpetrators. If it can be proved that A1 was the perpetrator and it is possible to infer that A2 provided indifferent encouragement or assistance during the offence by failing to take reasonable steps to intervene, and vice versa,[99] then both A1 and A2 can be convicted (under clause 2(1)) of encouraging or assisting an offence against the person, possibly murder.

A.83   Proving liability under clause 2(1) for encouraging or assisting murder would be difficult in many cases, however, because of the strict fault requirement imposed by clause 2(4)(b) in relation to the consequence element of the offence (death).

A.84   For this reason it would be advisable for the Crown to include on the indictment an alternative count of encouraging or assisting a non-fatal offence against the person,[100] although much will depend on the facts of the particular case.[101] It would also be advisable for the police to charge A1 and A2 with the alternative offence (or offences) under clause 1(1) or clause 2(1) when charging them with having committed the substantive offence as alleged perpetrators.

A.85   It is important to note that the focus for liability under Part 1, in cases where clause 10 is relied on, remains the offence D intended or expected rather than the offence which P actually committed. Thus, if D thought that P was going to kick their screaming child, V1, but P actually punched their quiet child, V2, D would be liable for his or her non-intervention in respect of V1 even though the actual principal offence was committed against V2. That said, in the sort of case described in our example, where D is present *during* P's commission of the principal offence against their child, V, and there is no difference between the offence in D's mind and the offence actually being committed, the issue will be of no practical importance. For this reason, in any such case we would expect the jury to be directed with reference to the principal offence actually committed by P.

Clause 11 – inability to do a particular criminal act
A.86   This clause has been explained above.[102]

Clause 12 – penalties
A.87   This clause is self-explanatory.

---

[99] The encouragement or assistance arises from A2's failure to take reasonable steps to discharge his or her parental duty to protect the child (see cl 15(2)(b)).

[100] For example, encouraging or assisting the offence of causing grievous bodily harm with intent to cause such harm, contrary to s 18 of the Offences Against the Person Act 1861.

[101] If there is no separate count on the indictment, the court may be able to rely on s 6(3)–(4) of the Criminal Law Act 1967 to convict D of a lesser (included) offence under Part 1 in cases where the jury is not satisfied that D committed the offence charged.

[102] See n 27 (para A.31) and n 62 (para A.47).

Part 4: CONSEQUENTIAL ALTERATIONS

Clause 13 – common law incitement

A.88   This clause is self-explanatory.

Clause 14 – amendments and repeals

A.89   Clause 14(1), with Part 1 of Schedule 3 to the Bill, provides that references in other statutory provisions to the common law offence of incitement are to be read as references to the offences in Part 1 of the Bill. This provision does not affect any statutory offence of incitement, such as the offence of soliciting murder.[103]

A.90   The other provisions in this clause are self-explanatory.

PART 5: INTERPRETATION

Clauses 15 and 16 – encouraging and assisting

A.91   The Bill does not contain a definition of conduct which is capable of encouraging or assisting. However, for the avoidance of doubt, clause 15 provides that conduct by D which is capable of encouraging or assisting a person to do a criminal act includes:

(1)   conduct which could encourage by putting pressure on someone (for example where D threatens another person);[104] and

(2)   conduct which could reduce the possibility of criminal proceedings being brought in respect of the act (such as the provision of advice to a person on how to avoid detection, or the provision of a gun to be used against any eye-witness).[105]

A.92   Clause 15(2)(b) provides, moreover, that a reference to a person's doing something which is capable of encouraging or assisting a person to do a criminal act can be a failure to take reasonable steps to discharge a relevant duty, for example where:

D (a security guard) fails to turn on a burglar alarm in order to assist another person's unauthorised entry as a burglar;

D (a mother) carries on watching television while her new partner (P) abuses her child.

A.93   The action D must take to avoid liability in the second example, where the encouragement or assistance is provided by an indifferent failure to exercise a duty, depends on all the circumstances. It is not an unduly onerous obligation, however, for D merely needs to take reasonable steps to discharge her duty.[106]

---

[103] Offences Against the Person Act 1861, s 4.

[104] Clause 15(1).

[105] Clause 15(2)(a).

[106] D's failure to discharge a duty will of course almost certainly be regarded as unreasonable if it was his purpose to encourage or assist another person to commit the principal offence, contrary to cl 1(1), as in the first example.

A.94   Clause 15(3) sets out a further limitation on the scope of liability for omissions, expressly providing that one particular type of omission – the failure to respond to a constable's request for assistance – is not encompassed by clause 15(2)(b).[107]

A.95   Clause 16 provides that if D1 arranges for another person (D2) to do something which has the capacity to encourage or assist another person to commit a criminal act, then D1 is also to be regarded as having done D2's act. Thus, a person such as a gang leader can be held liable for the encouragement or assistance provided by a member of his gang in carrying out his instructions.

Clause 17 – acts and criminal acts

A.96   Clause 17(1) provides that a reference to an act includes a reference to a course of conduct. This applies to D's own conduct[108] as well as any criminal act which D intends or believes will be committed by another person (for example, a course of conduct amounting to harassment).[109]

A.97   Clause 17(2) defines the term "criminal act", as explained above.[110]

A.98   Clause 17(3)(a) provides that a reference to the doing of a criminal act includes a reference to the continuation of an act which has already begun. This is illustrated by the second example given in paragraph A.41 where D, finding P in the act of committing rape, does an act (positioning himself to watch) which has the capacity to encourage the continuation of that offence by P.

A.99   Clause 17(3)(b) provides that a reference to the doing of a criminal act includes a reference to an attempt to do such an act. For example, D can be liable under clause 2(1) in relation to the principal offence of burglary if he sells P a jemmy in the belief that it will be used to attempt burglary, even though he believes that the attempt will fail.[111]

Clause 18 – intention

A.100   This clause provides, in effect, that the word "intention" as used in clause 1 of the Bill excludes the criminal law concept of foresight of a virtual certainty. In other words, references to D's intention are references to his purpose.

PART 6: FINAL PROVISIONS

A.101   Clauses 19 to 22 are self-explanatory.

---

[107] D's failure to provide a police officer with assistance when called upon to prevent a breach of the peace is itself a common law offence, but cl 15(3) ensures that D will not be liable under Part 1 of the Bill for any principal offence he believes will be committed (or intends should be committed) by his passive failure to help the police when called upon to provide assistance.

[108] D could be liable under Part 1 if he does a number of acts, none of which would be regarded as having the capacity to encourage or assist the doing of a criminal act, if the cumulative effect of D's course of conduct would be regarded as having the capacity to encourage or assist.

[109] Protection from Harassment Act 1997, s 1.

[110] Paras A.10 to A.19.

[111] If the principal offence in question is itself the offence of attempt, contrary to s 1 of the Criminal Attempts Act 1981, then cl 17(3)(b) is inapplicable. This explains the words in parentheses. It is to be noted that D can be liable under cl 1(1), but not cl 2(1) (or cl 2(2)), in relation to a principal offence of attempt (see cl 2(5)(b) and para 11 of sch 1).

Crime (Encouraging and Assisting) Bill

CONTENTS

A

B I L L

TO

To create offences in respect of the encouragement or assistance of crime; and to abolish the common law offence of incitement.

B E IT ENACTED by the Queen's most Excellent Majesty, by and with the advice and consent of the Lords Spiritual and Temporal, and Commons, in this present Parliament assembled, and by the authority of the same, as follows:—

PART 1

ENCOURAGING OR ASSISTING CRIME

1 Intentionally encouraging or assisting a criminal act

(1) A person commits an offence if—

    (a) he does an act capable of encouraging or assisting the doing of a criminal act in relation to an offence ("the principal offence"), and   5

    (b) he intends to encourage or assist the doing of that criminal act.

(2) If the principal offence requires proof of fault, a person is not guilty of an offence under this section unless—

    (a) he believes that, were another person to do the criminal act, that person would do it with the fault required for conviction of the principal offence, or   10

    (b) his state of mind is such that, were he to do the criminal act, he would do it with that fault.

(3) If particular circumstances or consequences (or both) must be proved for conviction of the principal offence, a person is not guilty of an offence under this section unless—   15

    (a) he intends the criminal act to be done—

        (i) in those circumstances,

        (ii) with those consequences, or   20

    (b) he believes that, were another person to do the criminal act, that person would do it—

        (i) in those circumstances,

           (ii)   with those consequences.

2   Encouraging or assisting criminal acts believing that one or more of them will be done

(1)   A person commits an offence if—
    (a)   he does an act capable of encouraging or assisting the doing of a criminal act (the "act in question"), and   *5*
    (b)   he believes—
        (i)   that the act in question will be done, and
        (ii)   that his act will encourage or assist the doing of the act in question.   *10*

(2)   A person commits an offence if—
    (a)   he does an act capable of encouraging or assisting the doing of one or more of a number of criminal acts, and
    (b)   he believes—
        (i)   that at least one of a number of criminal acts will be done (but has no belief as to which), and   *15*
        (ii)   that his act will encourage or assist the doing of one of those criminal acts ("the act in question").

(3)   If the principal offence requires proof of fault, a person is not guilty of an offence under this section unless—   *20*
    (a)   he believes that, were another person to do the act in question, that person would do it with the fault required for conviction of the principal offence, or
    (b)   his state of mind is such that, were he to do it, he would do it with that fault.   *25*

(4)   If particular circumstances or consequences (or both) must be proved for conviction of the principal offence, a person is not guilty of an offence under this section unless he believes that, were another person to do the act in question, that person would do it—
    (a)   in those circumstances,   *30*
    (b)   with those consequences.

(5)   Neither subsection (1) nor (2) applies if the principal offence is—
    (a)   an offence under this Part, or
    (b)   an offence listed in Schedule 1.

(6)   In this Act, in relation to an offence under subsection (1) or (2), "the principal offence" means the offence in relation to which the act in question is a criminal act.   *35*

3   Supplemental provisions

(1)   An offence may be committed under section 1 or 2 whether or not the principal offence is committed.   *40*

(2)   If a person's act is capable of encouraging or assisting the doing of a number of criminal acts—
    (a)   section 1 applies separately in relation to each act that he intends to encourage or assist to be done, and

    (b)   section 2(1) applies separately in relation to each act that he believes will be encouraged or assisted to be done.

(3)   A person may, in relation to the same act, commit both an offence under section 2(1) and an offence under section 2(2).

(4)   But a person may not, in relation to the same act, be prosecuted for more than one offence under section 2(2).

(5)   For the purposes of section 2(1)(b)(i) it is sufficient for the person concerned to believe that the act in question will be done if certain conditions are met.

(6)   For the purposes of section 2(2)(b)(i) it is sufficient for the person concerned to believe that one or more of the criminal acts will be done if certain conditions are met.

(7)   If a person is charged with an offence under section 2(2), both the act in question and the principal offence must be specified in the information, charge or indictment.

PART 2

DEFENCES AND OTHER LIMITATION ON LIABILITY

Defences

4   Defence of acting to prevent commission of offence etc.

A person is not guilty of an offence under section 1 or 2 if he proves that—
    (a)   he acted for the purpose of—
        (i)   preventing the commission of that offence or another offence, or
        (ii)   preventing, or limiting, the occurrence of harm, and
    (b)   it was reasonable for him to act as he did.

5   Defence of acting reasonably

(1)   A person is not guilty of an offence under section 2 if he proves—
    (a)   that he knew certain circumstances existed, and
    (b)   that it was reasonable for him to act as he did in those circumstances.

(2)   A person is not guilty of an offence under section 2 if he proves—
    (a)   that he believed certain circumstances to exist,
    (b)   that his belief was reasonable, and
    (c)   that it was reasonable for him to act as he did in the circumstances as he believed them to be.

Limitation on liability imposed under Part 1

6   Protective offences: victims not liable

(1)   A person is not guilty of an offence under section 1 or 2 if—
    (a)   the principal offence is a protective offence,
    (b)   he falls within the protected category, and

(c)   he is the person in respect of whom the principal offence was committed (or would have been if it had been committed).

(2)   "Protective offence" means an offence that exists (wholly or in part) for the protection of a particular category of persons ("the protected category").

PART 3

JURISDICTION AND PROCEDURE

7   Jurisdiction

(1)   If a person (D) knows or believes that what he anticipates might take place wholly or partly in England or Wales, he may be guilty of an offence under Part 1 no matter where he was at any relevant time.

(2)   If it is not proved that D knows or believes that what he anticipates might take place wholly or partly in England or Wales, he is not guilty of an offence under Part 1 unless paragraph 1, 2 or 3 of Schedule 2 applies.

(3)   In relation to an offence under section 1, a reference in this section (and in any of those paragraphs) to what D anticipates is a reference to the act, circumstances and consequences mentioned in subsections (2) and (3) of that section.

(4)   In relation to an offence under section 2, a reference in this section (and in any of those paragraphs) to what D anticipates is a reference to the act, circumstances and consequences mentioned in subsections (3) and (4) of that section.

8   Role of the Attorney General

No proceedings for an offence triable by reason of any provision of Schedule 2 may be instituted except by, or with the consent of, the Attorney General.

9   Mode of trial

The mode of trial of a person charged with an offence under Part 1 is to be determined as if he had been charged with the principal offence.

10   Persons who may be perpetrators or encouragers etc.

(1)   In proceedings for an offence under section 1 or 2 ("the Part 1 offence") the defendant may be convicted if—
    (a)   it is proved that he must have committed the Part 1 offence or the principal offence in question, but
    (b)   it is not proved which of those offences he committed.

(2)   For the purposes of subsection (1)(a), a person is not to be treated as having committed the principal offence merely because he aided, abetted, counselled or procured its commission.

11   Conviction under Part 1 not prevented by inability to do particular act

For the purposes of sections 1(2)(b) and 2(3)(b), the person concerned is to be assumed to be able to do the criminal act in question.

149

12   Penalties

(1)   This section applies if a person is convicted of an offence under Part 1.

(2)   If the principal offence is murder, he is liable to imprisonment for life.

(3)   Unless an enactment provides otherwise, he is liable in any other case to any
penalty for which he would be liable on conviction of the principal offence.   *5*

PART 4

CONSEQUENTIAL ALTERATIONS OF THE LAW

13   Abolition of common law replaced by this Act

The common law offence of inciting the commission of another offence is
abolished.   *10*

14   Consequential amendments and repeals

(1)   In the provisions listed in Part 1 of Schedule 3, any reference however
expressed to (or to conduct amounting to) the offence abolished by section 13
has effect as a reference to (or to conduct amounting to) the offences in Part 1
of this Act.   *15*

(2)   Part 2 of Schedule 3 contains other minor and consequential amendments.

(3)   The Secretary of State may by order –
    (a)   amend Part 1 of Schedule 3 by adding or removing a provision;
    (b)   amend any Act or subordinate legislation in such way as he thinks fit
in consequence of the provisions of this Act.   *20*

(4)   An order under subsection (3) –
    (a)   must be made by statutory instrument, and
    (b)   may not be made unless a draft of it has been laid before Parliament and
approved by a resolution of each House of Parliament.

(5)   Schedule 4 contains repeals.   *25*

PART 5

INTERPRETATION

15   Being capable of encouraging or assisting

(1)   A reference in this Act to a person's doing an act that is capable of encouraging
the doing of a criminal act includes a reference to his doing so by threatening   *30*
another person or otherwise putting pressure on another person to do the act.

(2)   A reference in this Act to a person's doing an act that is capable of encouraging
or assisting the doing of a criminal act includes a reference to his doing so by –
    (a)   taking steps to reduce the possibility of criminal proceedings being
brought in respect of the act's being done,   *35*
    (b)   failing to take reasonable steps to discharge a duty.

(3)   But a person is not to be regarded as doing an act that is capable of encouraging or assisting the doing of a criminal act merely because he fails to respond to a constable's request for assistance in preventing a breach of the peace.

16   Indirectly encouraging or assisting

If a person (D1) arranges for a person (D2) to do an act that is capable of   5
encouraging or assisting an act to be done, and D2 does any such act, D1 is also
to be treated for the purposes of this Act as having done it.

17   Acts and criminal acts

(1)   A reference in this Act to an act includes a reference to a course of conduct and
a reference to doing an act is to be read accordingly.   10

(2)   A reference in this Act to a criminal act is, in relation to an offence, a reference
to an act (or a failure to act) that falls within the definition of the act (or failure
to act) that must be proved in order for a person to be convicted of the offence.

(3)   A reference in this Act to the doing of a criminal act includes a reference to —
      (a)   the continuation of an act that has already begun;   15
      (b)   an attempt to do an act (except in relation to an offence of attempting to
            commit another offence).

18   Intention required for liability under section 1

(1)   A person is not to be taken to have intended to encourage or assist a criminal
act to be done merely because such encouragement or assistance was a   20
foreseeable consequence of his act.

(2)   A person is not to be taken to have intended that a criminal act be done in
particular circumstances or with particular consequences merely because its
being done in those circumstances or with those consequences was a
foreseeable consequence of his act.   25

(3)   A reference to a person's act is to an act of his of the kind mentioned in section
1(1)(a).

PART 6

FINAL PROVISIONS

19   Saving for offences committed before commencement   30

(1)   Nothing in this Act affects the operation of —
      (a)   any rule of the common law, or
      (b)   any provision of an Act or of subordinate legislation,
      in relation to offences committed wholly or partly before commencement.

(2)   An offence is partly committed before commencement if —   35
      (a)   a relevant event occurs before commencement; and
      (b)   another relevant event occurs on or after commencement.

(3)   "Commencement" means the day on which Part 1 comes into force.

(4)   "Relevant event", in relation to an offence, means any act or other event (including any consequence of an act) proof of which is required for conviction of the offence.

20   Commencement

This Act, except this section and sections 21 and 22, comes into force in accordance with provision made by the Secretary of State by order made by statutory instrument.

5

21   Extent

(1)   Subject to subsection (2), this Act extends to England and Wales only.

(2)   The following provisions of this Act also extend to Scotland and Northern Ireland —

10

    (a)   paragraphs 37 and 38 of Schedule 3 (and section 14(2) so far as it relates to those paragraphs);

    (b)   section 14(3) and (4);

    (c)   this Part.

15

22   Short title

This Act may be cited as the Crime (Encouraging and Assisting) Act 2006.

SCHEDULES

SCHEDULE 1

Section 2(5)(b)

OFFENCES TO WHICH SECTION 2 DOES NOT APPLY

PART 1

OFFENCES UNDER PARTICULAR ENACTMENTS

5

Offences against the Person Act 1861 (c. 100)

1   An offence under section 4 of the Offences against the Person Act 1861 (solicitation etc. of murder).

Public Meeting Act 1908 (c. 66)

2   An offence under section 1(2) of the Public Meeting Act 1908 (inciting others   10
to commit offences under that section).

Perjury Act 1911 (c. 6)

3   An offence under section 7(2) of the Perjury Act 1911 (inciting a person to commit an offence under that Act).

Aliens Restriction (Amendment) Act 1919 (c. 92)   15

4   An offence under section 3(1) of the Aliens Restriction (Amendment) Act 1919 (acts calculated or likely to cause sedition or disaffection amongst HM forces etc.).

5   An offence under section 3(2) of that Act (promoting or attempting to promote industrial unrest).   20

Official Secrets Act 1920 (c. 75)

6   An offence under section 7 of the Official Secrets Act 1920 (soliciting etc. commission of an offence under that Act or the Official Secrets Act 1911).

Incitement to Disaffection Act 1934 (c. 56)

7   An offence under section 1 of the Incitement to Disaffection Act 1934   25
(endeavouring to seduce members of HM forces from their duty or allegiance).

Crime (Encouraging and Assisting) Bill
Schedule 1 — Offences to which section 2 does not apply
Part 1 — Offences under particular enactments

9

Criminal Law Act 1967 (c. 58)

8   An offence under section 4(1) of the Criminal Law Act 1967 (assisting persons who have committed an offence).

9   An offence under section 5(1) of that Act (accepting or agreeing to accept consideration for not disclosing information about an offence).

Criminal Law Act 1977 (c. 45)

10   An offence under section 1(1) of the Criminal Law Act 1977 (conspiracy).

Criminal Attempts Act 1981 (c. 47)

11   An offence under section 1(1) of the Criminal Attempts Act 1981 (attempting to commit an offence).

Representation of the People Act 1983 (c. 2)

12   An offence under section 97(1) of the Representation of the People Act 1983 (public meetings) consisting in the incitement of others to act in a disorderly manner for the purpose of preventing at a lawful public meeting to which that section applies the transaction of the business for which the meeting was called.

Public Order Act 1986 (c. 64)

13   An offence under section 12(6) of the Public Order Act 1986 (inciting commission of offences under section 12(5) of that Act).

14   An offence under section 13(8) of that Act (inciting commission of offences under section 13(7) of that Act).

15   An offence under section 14(6) of that Act (inciting commission of offences under section 14(5) of that Act).

16   An offence under section 14B(3) of that Act (inciting commission of offences under section 14B(2) of that Act).

Terrorism Act 2000 (c. 11)

17   An offence under section 59 of the Terrorism Act 2000 (inciting in England and Wales the commission of acts of terrorism outside the United Kingdom).

PART 2

OTHER OFFENCES

18   An offence of conspiracy falling within section 5(2) or (3) of the Criminal Law Act 1977 (forms of conspiracy not affected by abolition of offence of conspiracy at common law).

19 (1) An attempt under a special statutory provision.

    (2) Sub-paragraph (1) is to be read with section 3 of the Criminal Attempts Act 1981.

SCHEDULE 2   Section 7(2)

EXTRA-TERRITORIALITY

1   (1) This paragraph applies if —

       (a) any relevant behaviour of D's takes place wholly or partly in England or Wales,

       (b) D knows or believes that what he anticipates might take place wholly or partly in a place outside England and Wales, and

       (c) either —

             (i) the principal offence is one that would be triable under the law of England and Wales if it were committed in that place, or

             (ii) if there are relevant conditions, it would be so triable if it were committed there by a person who satisfies the conditions.

     (2) "Relevant condition" means a condition that —

       (a) determines (wholly or in part) whether an offence committed outside England and Wales is nonetheless triable under the law of England and Wales, and

       (b) relates to the citizenship, nationality or residence of the person who commits it.

2   (1) This paragraph applies if —

       (a) paragraph 1 does not apply,

       (b) any relevant behaviour of D's takes place wholly or partly in England or Wales,

       (c) D knows or believes that what he anticipates might take place wholly or partly in a place outside England and Wales, and

       (d) what D anticipates would amount to an offence under the law in force in that place.

     (2) The condition in sub-paragraph (1)(d) is to be taken to be satisfied unless, not later than rules of court may provide, the defence serve on the prosecution a notice —

       (a) stating that on the facts as alleged the condition is not in their opinion satisfied,

       (b) showing their grounds for that opinion, and

       (c) requiring the prosecution to show that it is satisfied.

     (3) The court, if it thinks fit, may permit the defence to require the prosecution to show that the condition is satisfied without prior service of a notice under sub-paragraph (2).

     (4) In the Crown Court, the question whether the condition is satisfied is to be decided by the judge alone.

     (5) An act punishable under the law in force in any place outside England and Wales constitutes an offence under that law for the purposes of this paragraph, however it is described in that law.

3   This paragraph applies if —

       (a) any relevant behaviour of D's takes place wholly outside England and Wales,

    (b)   D knows or believes that what he anticipates might take place wholly or partly in a place outside England and Wales, and

    (c)   D could be tried under the law of England and Wales if he committed the principal offence in that place.

SCHEDULE 3

14(1) and (2)   *5*

MINOR AND CONSEQUENTIAL AMENDMENTS

PART 1

REFERENCES TO COMMON LAW OFFENCE OF INCITEMENT

1   Section 1B(2) of the Biological Weapons Act 1974 (c. 6) (Revenue and Customs prosecutions).   *10*

2   Section 17(1) of the Industry Act 1975 (c. 68) (no criminal proceedings to lie in respect of contravention of a prohibition order).

3   In the Magistrates' Courts Act 1980 (c. 43) —

    (a)   section 22(11)(b) (aggregation of value in relation to charges involving two or more scheduled offences);   *15*

    (b)   section 103(2)(d) (written statement of child admissible in committal proceedings for certain offences);

    (c)   paragraph 2 of Schedule 2 (offences for which the value involved is relevant to the mode of trial).

4   In the Betting and Gaming Duties Act 1981 (c. 63) —   *20*

    (a)   section 9(5) (prohibitions for protection of revenue);

    (b)   section 9A(4) (prohibitions for protection of revenue: overseas brokers).

5   Section 32(1)(b) of the Criminal Justice Act 1982 (c. 48) (early release of prisoners).   *25*

6   Section 80(3)(c) of the Police and Criminal Evidence Act 1984 (c. 60) (compellability of accused's spouse or civil partner).

7   Section 49(4) of the Airports Act 1986 (c. 31) (no criminal proceedings to lie in respect of contravention of compliance order).

8   Section 12(6)(a) of the Outer Space Act 1986 (c. 38) (offences).   *30*

9   Section 30(4) of the Gas Act 1986 (c. 44) (no criminal proceedings to lie in respect of contravention of final or provisional order).

10   Section 7(1) of the Public Order Act 1986 (c. 64) (consent of DPP to prosecution).

11   Section 2(3)(ba) of the Ministry of Defence Police Act 1987 (c. 4) (jurisdiction of members of MoD police).   *35*

12   In the Road Traffic Offenders Act 1988 (c. 53) —

    (a)   section 28(2) (penalty points to be attributed to an offence);

    (b)   section 34(5) (disqualification for certain offences);

156

12   *Crime (Encouraging and Assisting) Bill*
Schedule 3 — Minor and consequential amendments
Part 1 — References to common law offence of incitement

(c)   section 35(5A) (disqualification for repeated offences).

13   Paragraph 2(a) of Schedule 1 to the Football Spectators Act 1989 (c. 37) (offences).

14   In the Aviation and Maritime Security Act 1990 (c. 31) —
    (a)   section 11(3)(b) (destroying ships or fixed platforms or endangering   *5*
        their safety);
    (b)   section 15(2)(c) (master's power of delivery).

15   Section 53(7) of the Criminal Justice Act 1991 (c. 53) (cases involving children in which notice of transfer may be given).

16   In the Sexual Offences (Amendment) Act 1992 (c. 34) —   *10*
    (a)   section 2(1)(g)(offences to which Act applies);
    (b)   section 6(2A) (person who is to be treated as person against whom inchoate offences are committed).

17   Section 12(7) of the Finance Act 1994 (c. 9) (offences of fraud and dishonesty).   *15*

18   Paragraph (b) of the definition of "specified offence" in section 60(6) of the Drug Trafficking Act 1994 (c. 37) (Revenue and Customs prosecutions).

19   Section 30A(2) of the Chemical Weapons Act 1996 (c. 6) (Revenue and Customs prosecutions).

20   Section 14(2)(d) of the Northern Ireland (Sentences) Act 1998 (c. 35)   *20*
(inadmissibility).

21   Section 51C(3)(e) of the Crime and Disorder Act 1998 (c. 37) (notices in certain cases involving children).

22   Section 62(2) of the Youth Justice and Criminal Evidence Act 1999 (c. 23) (meaning of "sexual offence" and other references to offences).   *25*

23   Section 147(2) of the Powers of Criminal Courts (Sentencing) Act 2000 (c. 6) (driving disqualification where vehicle used for purposes of crime).

24   Paragraph 3(t)(i) of Schedule 4 to the Criminal Justice and Court Services Act 2000 (c. 43) (meaning of "offence against a child").

25   Section 34(1)(g) of the Criminal Justice and Police Act 2001 (c. 16) (meaning   *30*
of "drug trafficking offence").

26   Section 55(1)(b) of the International Criminal Court Act 2001 (c. 17) (meaning of "ancillary offence").

27   Section 53(2) of the Anti-terrorism, Crime and Security Act 2001 (c. 24) (Revenue and Customs prosecutions).   *35*

28   In the Proceeds of Crime Act 2002 (c. 29) —
    (a)   section 340(11)(b) (interpretation of Part 7: money laundering);
    (b)   section 415(2)(a) (money laundering offences for purposes of Part 8: investigations);
    (c)   section 447(9)(b) (interpretation of Part 11: national and international   *40*
        co-operation);
    (d)   section 451(6)(c) (Revenue and Customs prosecutions);
    (e)   paragraph 10 of Schedule 2 (lifestyle offences: England and Wales).

Crime (Encouraging and Assisting) Bill
Schedule 3 — Minor and consequential amendments
Part 1 — References to common law offence of incitement

13

29   Section 4 of the Dealing in Cultural Objects (Offences) Act 2003 (c. 27) (Revenue and Customs prosecutions).

30   Section 142(7)(a) of the Extradition Act 2003 (c. 41) (extradition from category 1 territory to the United Kingdom).

31   Paragraph 3(a) of Schedule 2 to the Sexual Offences Act 2003 (c. 42) (sexual offences to which section 72 of that Act applies).

32   In Schedule 15 to the Criminal Justice Act 2003 (c. 44) (specified violent and sexual offences for the purposes of Chapter 5 of Part 12 of that Act) —
    (a)   paragraph 64(a);
    (b)   paragraph 153(a).

33   Section 14 of the Gangmasters (Licensing) Act 2004 (c. 11) (enforcement officer's power of arrest).

PART 2

OTHER MINOR AND CONSEQUENTIAL AMENDMENTS

Criminal Law Act 1977 (c. 45)

34   In section 5 of the Criminal Law Act 1977 (effects of creation of statutory offence of conspiracy), omit subsection (7).

Computer Misuse Act 1990 (c. 18)

35   (1)   The Computer Misuse Act 1990 is amended as follows.

    (2)   In section 6 (incitement), omit subsection (3).

    (3)   In section 7 (territorial scope of inchoate offences related to offences under external law corresponding to offences under the Act), omit subsection (4).

    (4)   In section 8(2) (relevance of external law), omit "or by virtue of section 7(4) above".

    (5)   In section 9(2) (offences in relation to which British citizenship is immaterial), omit paragraph (d).

International Criminal Court Act 2001 (c. 17)

36   In section 55 of the International Criminal Court Act 2001 (meaning of ancillary offence), omit subsection (3).

Sexual Offences Act 2003

37   In Schedule 3 to the Sexual Offences Act 2003 (sexual offences for the purposes of Part 2 of that Act), after paragraph 94 insert —

    "94A   A reference in a preceding paragraph to an offence ("offence A") includes a reference to an offence under the Crime (Encouraging and Assisting) Act 2006 in relation to which offence A is the principal offence."

38   In Schedule 5 to that Act (other offences which are relevant for the purposes

14

Crime (Encouraging and Assisting) Bill
Schedule 3 — Minor and consequential amendments
Part 2 — Other minor and consequential amendments

of Part 2 of the Act), after paragraph 173 insert—

> "173A   A reference in a preceding paragraph to an offence ("offence A") includes a reference to an offence under the Crime (Encouraging and Assisting) Act 2006 in relation to which offence A is the principal offence."

Serious Organised Crime and Police Act 2005 (c. 15)

39   In section 136 of the Serious Organised Crime and Police Act 2005 (penalties in relation to demonstrations in the vicinity of Parliament), for subsection (4) substitute—

> "(4)   A person who is guilty of an offence under the Crime (Encouraging and Assisting) Act 2005 in relation to which an offence mentioned in subsection (1), (2) or (3) is the principal offence, is liable on summary conviction to imprisonment for a term not exceeding 51 weeks, to a fine not exceeding level 4 on the standard scale or to both."

SCHEDULE 4   14(5)

REPEALS

Short title and chapter	Extent of repeal
Criminal Law Act 1977 (c. 45)	Section 5(7).
Computer Misuse Act 1990 (c. 18)	Section 6(3).
	Section 7(4).
	In section 8(3), the words "or by virtue of section 7(4) above".
	Section 9(2)(d).
International Criminal Court Act 2001 (c. 17)	Section 55(3).

APPENDIX B
SUICIDES: AIDED OR ASSISTED?

INTRODUCTION

B.1 Over recent years there has been a growth in the phenomenon of "suicide websites". In their least objectionable form such websites provide the visitor with little more than advice as to potential methods for committing suicide. However, such websites can also offer services akin to a dating agency for potential suicides. Such websites have been at the root of numerous suicide pacts, uniting people contemplating suicide and providing them with the advice as to how they should end their lives. This has become an increasing cause for concern.[1]

B.2 In the light of this, any review of offences of "encouraging and assisting" needs to consider the issue of assisting suicide. Currently the law's response to the problem of assisting suicide is found in section 2 of the Suicide Act 1961,[2] which makes it an offence to "aid, abet, counsel or procure the suicide of another, or an attempt by another to commit suicide".[3] The question is whether involvement in the suicide of another ought to continue to be criminalised under section 2 of the Suicide Act or whether the behaviour ought to be addressed by the Crime (Encouraging and Assisting) Bill.[4]

B.3 This Appendix will start by explaining why the offence of aiding suicide under section 2 of the Suicide Act, in the absence of any reform, offers an adequate solution to the problem posed by those who involve themselves in the suicide of another. It will then explore some potential benefits of moving such behaviour within the scope of the Encouraging and Assisting Bill in any event.

---

[1] *Web 'may fuel suicide pact rise'* – 2 December 2005, http://news.bbc.co.uk/1/hi/health/4061623.stm; *Coroner's anger at suicide site* – 15 August 2003, http://news.bbc.co.uk/1/hi/wales/south_east/3154835.stm.

[2] Hereafter "the Suicide Act".

[3] Hereafter "aiding suicide".

[4] Hereafter "the Encouraging and Assisting Bill".

RETAINING THE OFFENCE UNDER SECTION 2 SUICIDE ACT 1961

B.4   As we explained in Part 3,[5] the biggest problem that the Encouraging and Assisting Bill seeks to address is that there is secondary, that is derivative, liability for aiding crime but no inchoate liability for assisting crime.[6] Therefore, if the principal offence that the assistor intends to assist never comes about the assistor is not liable for any offence at all. This is in stark contrast to encouragers who are guilty of the inchoate offence of incitement in the absence of the encouraged principal offence being committed. There is no good reason for this differential treatment of assistors and encouragers, especially given the fact that the line between assisting and encouraging is both hazy and hard to draw.

B.5   However, the problem posed by the lack of an inchoate offence of assisting to complement secondary liability as an assistor would be rendered academic if it were possible to convict of an "attempt to aid, abet, counsel or procure". However, no such offence is known to English law, as section 1(4)(b) of the Criminal Attempts Act 1981[7] expressly states that there shall be no offence of attempting to aid abet counsel or procure.[8] Therefore, the absence of an inchoate offence of assisting leaves a genuine gap in the law which the Encouraging and Assisting Bill seeks to fill.

B.6   However, this gap in the law does not affect the offence of aiding suicide. This is because of the special nature of the offence of aiding suicide contrary to section 2 of the Suicide Act. This offence, despite being drafted in the language of secondary liability, is in fact an offence committed by the defendant as a principal rather than as a secondary party. This is because in cases of aiding suicide the aided party commits no crime from which the secondary liability of the aider could be derived. Therefore, those who aid suicide have to be convicted as the principal offender of the offence of aiding suicide rather than being convicted of suicide committed as a secondary participant.

B.7   This has important consequences. Prior to the passing of the Suicide Act, suicide was an offence which could be aided by a secondary party but there could be no attempt to aid. The passage of the Suicide Act altered the situation: aiding suicide became a statutory offence committed as a principal that could be attempted like any other offence.

---

[5]   Paras 3.2 to 3.17 above.

[6]   "Aid, abet, counsel or procure" is the term used in s 8 of the Accessories and Abettors Act 1861 and is the language of secondary liability. Encourage or Assist is the term used in the Encouraging and Assisting Bill and is the language of inchoate liability. Generally, "aid" and "abet" are synonymous with "assist", whilst "counsel" means "encourage", with "procure" being an anomalous "niche" form of secondary liability. Hereafter, unless the context otherwise dictates, "assisting" will be used as a synonym for "assisting and encouraging" and "aiding" will be used as a synonym for "aiding, abetting, counselling, and procuring".

[7]   Hereafter "the Criminal Attempts Act".

[8]   It appears that the decision not to have an offence of attempting to aid and abet seems to be based on the view that instances of attempting to aid and abet whereby the potential defendant fails to be helpful are too remote from the harm caused by the principal offence to be criminalised. However, there was no discussion of the situation where the potential defendant manages to be helpful but there fails to be a principal offence from which his liability could be derived. See Attempt, and Impossibility in Relation to Attempt, Conspiracy and Incitement (1980) Law Com 102.

The law on aiding suicide contrary to section 2 of the Suicide Act

B.8 Currently there are two major authorities on aiding suicide contrary to section 2 of the Suicide Act or attempting to do the same: *Attorney General v Able*[9] and *R v S*.[10] Each is worthy of brief consideration.

Able

B.9 The leading authority on aiding suicide contrary to section 2 of the Suicide Act is *Able*. In *Able* the Attorney General sought a High Court declaration that the Voluntary Euthanasia Society's distribution of a booklet entitled "A guide to self-deliverance", which contained advice as to five recommended methods of committing suicide, was unlawful. The application for declaratory relief was focussed on the offence of aiding suicide contrary to section 2 of the Suicide Act. No reliance appears to have been placed upon the offence of attempting to do the same contrary to section 1 of the Criminal Attempts Act.

B.10 Mr Justice Woolf (as he then was) declined to grant the requested declaration. Having found that the option of granting the declaration was open to him in principle, he found on the facts that the Attorney General had not established that the supply of the booklet was necessarily an offence under section 2 of the Suicide Act.

B.11 However, the judgment is in some ways problematic. Two questions in particular warrant closer attention:

(1) What is the mens rea of the offence of aiding suicide?

(2) What is the actus reus of the offence of attempting to aid suicide?

B.12 With regard to the first question, Mr Justice Woolf held:

> As a matter of principle, it seems to me that as long as there is the necessary intent to assist those who are contemplating suicide to commit suicide if they decide to do so, it does not matter that the supplier does not know the state of mind of the actual recipient.[11]

---

[9] [1984] QB 795.

[10] [2005] EWCA Crim 819.

[11] [1984] QB 795, 811.

B.13   This is a departure from the existing law on secondary liability, which suggests that the secondary party must *know* of all the "essential matters that constitute the offence".[12] It appears that the defendant need not know that the recipient has decided to commit suicide, or is even contemplating suicide. It appears to suffice that the defendant intends to assist the recipient to commit suicide should he decide to do so. Whilst this is a departure from the general law on secondary liability, as has already been pointed out the offence of aiding suicide is committed as a principal not as a secondary party. *Able* is therefore authoritative on this point.[13]

B.14   Turning to the second question, Mr Justice Woolf appears to contradict himself as to the actus reus of attempting to aid suicide contrary to section 1 of the Criminal Attempts Act. At one point Mr Justice Woolf seems to suggest that actual assistance is necessary even for the offence of attempting to aid suicide. In response to the submission that in some cases a recipient who was contemplating suicide may actually be deterred from doing so by reading the booklet and that it would be "quite nonsensical to regard the supply of the booklet as being an attempted offence contrary to section 2",[14] Mr Justice Woolf said:

> I agree … because, in such a case, the booklet has not provided any assistance with a view to a contemplated suicide. Such assistance is necessary to establish the actus reus for even the attempted offence.[15]

B.15   Immediately afterwards Mr Justice Woolf continued by saying that there would be cases where, for example, there had been a long delay between the supply of the booklet and the suicide, where:

> there would not be a sufficient connection between the attempted suicide and the supply of the booklet to make the supplier responsible.[16]

B.16   However, the idea that the actus reus of attempting to aid suicide should require actual assistance seems inconsistent with the general law of attempts. At another point, further down the same page, when Mr Justice Woolf came to summarising his conclusions, all reference to actual assistance being necessary for the actus reus of attempting to aid suicide disappears. He said that section 2 requires

---

[12]   *Johnston v Youden* [1950] 1 KB 544, 546, by Lord Chief Justice Goddard.

[13]   In any event, the rule that the secondary participant must *know* of all essential elements of the principal offence has been departed from in a range of cases (although no general principle can be derived from such cases) including: *Carter v Richardson* [1974] RTR 314 and *Blakely and Sutton v DPP* [1991] RTR 405.

[14]   [1984] QB 795, 811.

[15]   Above.

[16]   [1984] QB 795, 812.

(a) that the alleged offender had the necessary intent, that is, he intended the booklet to be used by someone contemplating suicide and intended that person would be assisted by the booklet's contents, or otherwise encouraged to attempt to take or to take his own life; (b) that while he still had that intention he distributed the booklet to such a person who read it; and, (c) in addition, if an offence under section 2 is to be proved, that such a person was assisted or encouraged by so reading the booklet to attempt to take or to take his own life, *otherwise the alleged offender cannot be guilty of more than an attempt.*[17]

B.17 This passage seems more compatible with the general law on attempts. At this point it is useful to consider *S*.

S

B.18 *S* is the leading authority on attempting to aid suicide contrary to section 1 of the Criminal Attempts Act. In *S* the defendant had encouraged his girlfriend to commit suicide. He had plied her with alcohol, dictated her suicide note, taken her to a jetty, and encouraged her to jump. The victim was found alive some time later at the bottom of the jetty. *S* was convicted of attempting to aid and abet suicide contrary to section 1 of the Criminal Attempts Act on facts that in essence amounted to encouraging or inciting someone who does not wish to commit suicide to do so.

B.19 On appeal it was held that the case was indeed one of attempting to aid suicide. Lord Justice Rix held that the offence of attempting to assist suicide did not require the person assisted to subsequently form an intention to commit suicide.[18] Indeed, he approved the direction that it was only the assistor's mind, and not the assistee's mind, which was relevant. In doing so he observed that if the assistee did not wish to commit suicide this merely rendered D's attempt to aid and abet suicide an attempt at the impossible, which was still a crime.[19]

B.20 If there can be an attempt to aid suicide in the absence of a subsequent decision by the assisted party to commit suicide, it follows that actual assistance does not form part of the actus reus of attempting to aid suicide. It was only the concluding paragraph from Mr Justice Woolf's judgment in *Able*, and not the more problematic paragraphs that preceded it, that were cited to the Court of Appeal in *S*.[20] Since the problematic passages in *Able* on attempting to aid suicide were strictly obiter, *S* authoritatively determines that no actual assistance need be given for there to be an attempt to aid suicide.

Conclusion on the current law of aiding or attempting to aid suicide

B.21 Therefore, there will be an offence of attempting to aid suicide contrary to section 1 of the Criminal Attempts Act where:

---

[17] [1984] 1 QB 795, 812 (emphasis added).

[18] [2005] EWCA Crim 819, [36] to [38].

[19] Above, [40].

[20] Above, [36].

(1)   the defendant does an act that is more than merely preparatory to aiding suicide; and

(2)   he does that act with an intention that those people aided by his act (who themselves intend to commit suicide or who go on to form the intention to commit suicide) will be aided in committing or attempting to commit suicide.

B.22   Moreover, the offence of aiding suicide contrary to section 2 of the Suicide Act will be committed if in addition to the above:

(1)   the recipient of the act intended to aid goes on to commit or attempt to commit suicide; and

(2)   he or she is in fact aided in doing so by the defendant's act.

Conclusion on retaining the offence of aiding suicide

B.23   In conclusion, it appears that the offences of aiding suicide and attempting to aid suicide together provide adequate coverage of all behaviour that ought to be unlawful. Had the Attorney General in *Able* relied on both section 2 of the Suicide Act *and* section 1 of the Criminal Attempts Act then he ought to have been granted the declaration he sought.

B.24   Moreover, in the context of suicide websites one factual point ought to be highlighted. In *Able* each supply of the booklet was a separate act which would have constituted a separate offence. This is in stark contrast to suicide websites. Here there is a single act, which happens to be able to supply assistance to a large number of people. The facts in *Able* would have only been comparable to a suicide website if the Society had taken out a billboard advert rather than sending copies of a booklet out to recipients on request. This is significant because to obtain a declaration in *Able* the Attorney General had to show that every act was a crime, that is that every sending of the booklet would be a crime.

B.25   Whilst in the case of a suicide website, the Attorney General would still need to show that every act was an offence, this is more easily done in the case of suicide websites as there is only one act, that of publishing the website. This single act can then be shown to constitute an offence contrary to the Criminal Attempts Act 1981, if the publisher has the requisite intention. It will also constitute an offence contrary to section 2 of the suicide act if it is shown that any one single visitor to the website was aided by the website to commit suicide.

B.26   Therefore, the contemporary problems posed by suicide websites and other involvements in the suicide of another could adequately be addressed without reform to section 2 of the Suicide Act. As such there is no need to supplement "secondary" liability for aiding suicide with an inchoate offence of assisting suicide.

THE CASE FOR REFORMING SECTION 2 OF THE SUICIDE ACT

B.27   However, there are options for the reform of section 2 of the Suicide Act that deserve serious consideration. Two potential changes are particularly attractive.

B.28   Firstly, there is a strong case for updating the language of section 2 of the Suicide Act.

B.29   Secondly, there is a strong case for applying the Encouraging and Assisting Bill's broader provisions on extra-territorial jurisdiction to the offence of aiding suicide contrary to section 2 of the Suicide Act. These provisions would be especially useful in combating suicide websites. This is because the Internet facilitates cross-border communication and its use is, therefore, by its very nature, more likely to raise jurisdictional issues.

Printed in the UK by The Stationery Office Limited
on behalf of the Controller of Her Majesty's Stationery Office
ID 5387063 07/06
Printed on Paper containing 75% post consumer waste and 25% ECF pulp.